HABITS

HABITS

why do you do what you do?

john nicholson

For my parents

First published 1977 by
Macmillan London Limited
London and Basingstoke
Associated companies in Delhi, Dublin,
Hong Kong, Johannesburg, Lagos, Melbourne,
New York, Singapore & Tokyo

British Library Cataloguing in Publication Data
Nicholson, John, b. 1945
  Habits.
  1. Habit
  I. Title
  152.3'3   BF335
  ISBN 0–333–22343–8

Printed in Great Britain by offset lithography by
Billing & Sons Ltd, Guildford, London and Worcester

Contents

Acknowledgements

Habits grew out of a series of articles on the psychology of everyday life which I wrote for *New Society*. I am very grateful to the magazine's editor, Paul Barker, whose idea the series was, and to Kate Loewenthal, my colleague at Bedford College, without whose help the articles would never have been written. Some of the material for the book came to my attention when I was an editorial consultant to the magazine *New Behaviour*, now sadly defunct, and I am indebted to its editor, Peter Evans, staff and contributors. Many people have given me specialist advice, including Margaret Christie, Max Coltheart, John Goodyear, Adam Hilton, Monica Lawlor, Fred Metcalf, Catherine Simmonds, John Ward and Marylin Williams. I am also very grateful to those who have read parts of the book in manuscript form: Max Coltheart, Jane Kalim, Caroline Lewis, Fred Metcalf, Kate Nicholson, Peter O'Donnell, David Robson and Clare Toynbee. It has been improved by their comments, although final responsibility is, of course, mine alone. I am indebted to all my colleagues in the Psychology Department at Bedford College, London University, not only for their advice and encouragement, but also for tolerating my dereliction of duty during the months while I was working on the book. Finally, it is a pleasure to acknowledge the contribution made by my editors, Michael Alcock, Kyle Cathie and Angela Dyer, and to thank Valerie White, who typed the manuscript.

Preface

You may not accept that the proper study of man is man, but human behaviour is a subject on which you probably hold strong views. Since psychology is the study of human behaviour, we are all psychologists, and most of us feel that we have a shrewd idea why we do what we do. However, do-it-yourself psychology has two flaws: your intuitions about your own behaviour may be wrong, and you can never be certain to what extent other people feel and react as you do.

The aim of this book is to examine some of our most familiar habits (according to the dictionary, habits are customary manners of acting, rather than compulsions) and to see how well popular beliefs about them stand up to scientific testing. Many of your theories will be confirmed, and you may be reassured to discover that other people share what you thought were your quirks. But sometimes laboratory experiments and controlled observation in real-life settings reveal that things are more complicated than they seem, and I shall be surprised if you finish the book without having to reconsider at least some of your fundamental beliefs about human nature.

Each chapter of *Habits* stands on its own, so the book can be read in any order. Related chapters have been grouped together, and move from habits which are obviously biological necessities to those which, at first glance, may appear to be luxuries or even harmful. Although there is also a movement throughout the book from the physiological to the applied, via experimental and social psychology, none of the habits discussed can be classed as, say, *either* physiological *or* social. Sleeping and eating, for example, are often thought of as purely physiological, but both have important sociological and anthropological aspects. The fact is that our habits do not fall tidily into the different areas in which psychologists specialise, and this may be one reason why human behaviour is still so incompletely understood.

Habits is written for readers without any prior technical knowledge of psychology, and there are only two chapters – those on eating and sleeping – where people without any scientific background whatsoever may find themselves briefly at a disadvantage. There are still enormous gaps in our understanding of human behaviour, but we know enough to be certain that no single approach to the subject is going to provide all the answers. We shall therefore be looking at evidence from fields as far apart as physiology and psychoanalysis, zoology and market research.

The book does not offer a new philosophy of living or a technique guaranteed to invest your life with meaning, but I hope to persuade you that the information which has been accumulated by experimental and applied psychologists over the hundred years or so during which behaviour has been studied scientifically has some bearing on our day to day existence, and that, where human behaviour is concerned, the obvious explanations are not always the right ones.

1 Living
with other people

The advantages of living in societies rather than in isolation are obvious and overwhelming. The willingness to live and work in groups, together with the uniquely elaborate organisation of the human cerebral cortex, gives us supremacy over all other species. Because we are prepared to pool talents and skills and to share amenities and resources, we can afford to be different from each other, and it is to this diversity that we owe the richness of our culture and our extraordinary inventiveness. But the fact that we *are* very different from each other frequently leads to misunderstandings and the disruption of social relations. Living with other people imposes certain restrictions on us as individuals, and in this chapter we shall be looking at some of the ways in which we are affected by having to deal with other people. Do you have needs as an individual which go unsatisfied as a result of having to rub shoulders with your fellow men? What costs do you incur by deciding to live with another person, as part of a group or family?

The need for elbow room
Since the publication in 1966 of Robert Ardrey's *The Territorial Imperative*, it has been widely accepted that people have an innate need for acquiring, maintaining and defending territory, comparable to their need for food and water. Ardrey based his claim largely on a comparison between the effectiveness of the American and Russian farming programmes, arguing that collective farming is relatively unsuccessful because a man who does not own the land he farms is denying his territorial need, and will therefore work less hard. Unfortunately for Ardrey, evidence from other countries such as Israel suggests that the collective ideal is not necessarily associated with inferior productivity.

9

Many *animals* engage in territorial behaviour – any reservations I might have about this are dispelled every time I look beyond my typewriter into the garden where my cat devotes most of her (admittedly few) waking hours to the defence of her patch – but I suspect that territoriality is much less of a force in *human* behaviour than Ardrey would have us believe. Like other students of animal behaviour – Desmond Morris and Konrad Lorenz, for example – Ardrey is too ready to make the assumption that what holds for other animals must necessarily hold for man. (A wit has said that the only difference between a conjuror and an ethologist is that one pulls rabbits out of a hat, the other habits out of a rat!) We may be animals, with habits which often betray their evolutionary origins, but as social beings and thinkers we are in a class of our own. It is perfectly fair to form hypotheses about human behaviour as a result of observing what animals do, but hazardous to apply laws governing animal behaviour directly to human actions, without first checking that men and animals do actually share the behaviour in question. Even when this seems to be the case, there is no guarantee that apparently identical behaviour has the same function in different species.

It seems likely that our need for territory – which may threaten our effectiveness as social agents – has over the centuries become progressively less potent as our social instinct has increased. This idea is supported by the results of an experiment on social isolation, in which volunteers (naval ratings) spent ten days in a confined space, in pairs but deprived of all other company. They became increasingly unsociable and, at the same time, more insistent that a particular chair or side of the table was 'theirs'. These findings suggest that when we artificially reduce a person's scope for social behaviour he becomes more territorial, and that although our need for territory may be relatively insignificant under normal conditions, it is dormant rather than extinct.

For animals, the possession of territory can offer safety and security; man can rely on the institutions of society to satisfy both these needs, as part of what Rousseau called the social contract. It is no longer necessary to be lord of the manor or king of the castle. The need to own property is far from being a universal characteristic. True, the British still seem prepared to go to almost any lengths to own the houses in which they live, but this behaviour is considered eccentric by their near neighbours the French.

I have emphasised the dangers of extrapolating from animal to human behaviour where territoriality is concerned, but I now have to admit that the concept of *personal space*, which has inspired the most revealing insights into human territorial requirements, owes its origins to the study of animal behaviour. It was the observation that individual animals seem to be extremely sensitive to the distance separating them from their fellows which suggested that each animal might be surrounded by a series of spatial zones (its territory), into which it allowed others to intrude only on certain occasions. The anthropologist Edward Hall was the first to apply this notion to humans – he coined the term *proxemics* to describe the scientific study of human spatial behaviour – and his observations powerfully supported the idea that we too have definite views about where we want other people in relation to ourselves. It is as if everyone were surrounded by a portable bubble of space, which can be divided into a series of concentric globes, each of which represents the region in which we are happy to tolerate the presence of another person in a particular situation.

The rules governing our different spatial requirements are so strict that by observing two people from a distance we can make an accurate guess about the nature of their relationship, based solely on the amount of space separating them. As we shall see, there are significant cultural and individual differences in spatial requirements, but each person is strikingly consistent in his proxemic behaviour. A diagram of the social interaction areas of a typical, middle-class, adult native of the north-eastern seaboard of the United States, based on Hall's findings, illustrates this well (see p. 12).

Each zone may be divided into a close and a far phase. The close phase of the *intimate zone* extends six inches from a person's body, and is reserved for the closest encounters – making love and wrestling, for example; the far phase (6 to 18 inches from the body) is the scene of interactions in which touching is permitted and conversation takes place in a whisper.

11

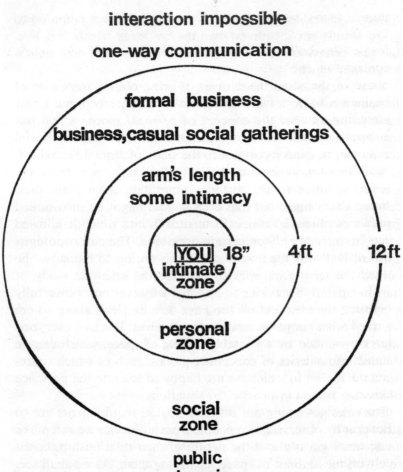

interaction impossible

one-way communication

formal business

business, casual social gatherings

arm's length
some intimacy

YOU 18"   4ft   12ft
intimate
zone

personal
zone

social
zone

public
domain

Sometimes intimate space is unavoidably violated by a non-intimate – in a crowded lift or train – in which case we go to great pains to show that the appearance of intimacy is an illusion. We stand rigid and immobile, studiously avoiding catching the other person's eye, and generally demonstrating that though they may be near us, they are not actually with us: our unease reflects the power of the rules of proxemics which are being broken, rather than actual physical discomfort.

The *personal zone* is reserved for casual encounters. In the near phase (18 inches to 2½ feet) there is still an implication of

12

intimacy, say between parent and child or very close friends. The far phase ($2\frac{1}{2}$ to 4 feet) is a suitable conversational distance for people who know each other but have no desire for physical contact; we use it to 'keep people at arm's length'. The close phase of the *social zone* (4 to 7 feet) may be described as a business distance: it is for people who work together, or who are attending a casual social gathering. The far phase (7 to 12 feet) is appropriate for more formal occasions – interviews, for example, or business negotiations. Beyond twelve feet lies the *public domain*. In the close phase (12 to 25 feet) communication is formal and usually one-way: we are addressing an audience rather than engaging in social interaction. The far phase of the public domain – a distance from ourselves of more than 25 feet – can be exploited to avoid conversation: so long as we maintain this distance, we are safe. We watch plays from this far away in a conventional theatre; 'intimate theatre' brings the audience within it, with the intention of creating genuine interaction between actors and audience.

Hall's mapping-out of personal space, which was based largely on observation, has been fairly rigorously tested, and it stands up well. Social psychologists have been particularly concerned to identify differences in spatial requirements between cultures. For example, it has been found that Arabs are more direct in their proxemic behaviour than North Americans and Europeans. They stand closer together, are more apt to touch one another, and look each other squarely in the eye while conversing in (to Western ears) ringing tones. There is also empirical evidence that they prefer to deal with foreigners who have been trained to adopt Arab proxemic norms – a point that export salesmen might profitably bear in mind. But it would be unwise to make too much of these national differences, for there are very striking differences in spatial behaviour between people of the same nationality, and regional and cultural variations often seem to make nonsense of national stereotypes. For example, the British are usually regarded as a stand-offish race. My colleague Dr Kate Loewenthal was therefore surprised while travelling around rural areas of Wales to observe that, on the occasions when she was the only passenger in a bus, anyone joining the bus would make a point of coming and sharing a double seat with her, to the discomfort of them both, while the rest of the seats remained empty!

Probably the most extreme set of cultural proxemic rules is that of the traditional caste system which still operates in rural areas of India. Members of the lowest of the five major castes – Nayadis (untouchables) – must not come within 64 feet of a Cheruman, who in turn must maintain a distance of 32 feet from an Iravan. Iravans are not allowed within 25 feet of a Nayar, who himself must come no closer than seven feet from a Brahmin. Since these distances are additive, an untouchable must never come within 128 feet of a Brahmin. This is an artificial, largely symbolic system of rules, but even in less traditional cultures certain types of people have unusually large personal space requirements. Studies carried out in America and South Africa show that people who have been convicted of crimes of violence need a much larger *body-buffer zone* than those convicted of non-violent crimes, not only while they are in prison but when they are back in the outside world. A person's body-buffer zone is defined as the point at which he begins to feel uncomfortable when someone walks towards him, and more detailed investigation has shown that this subjective feeling of discomfort is accompanied by an increase in physiological arousal. Similar research has shown that schizophrenic patients require an abnormally large pocket of personal space.

Variations in spatial requirements take many less dramatic forms. It is generally found that women need less personal space than men, that we stand closer to a member of the opposite sex, and – as Hall's analysis would predict – that friends converse at closer quarters than strangers. It is also clear that status confers the right to more personal space. The more important an executive is, the fewer equals or intimates he will have in the company, and the more time he will spend talking *at* people rather than *with* them. This he can do from behind a desk large enough to prevent anyone getting closer than his social zone. He leaves its security only to confer with equals, in a different part of the room where there are more intimate seating arrangements. The connection between personal space and status offers great scope to anyone interested in the practice of

14

oneupmanship. If you suspect that someone is about to try and assert his superiority over you from behind an enormous desk, don't take the chair he offers: this will put you in the position of being interviewed. Instead, try walking right up to the desk and then assume a casual pose on the edge of it. By doing so, you will simultaneously have asserted your right to violate his personal space (thereby claiming that you are his superior), and belittled the importance of his work by treating his working area as a suitable place to park your behind. You will also have gained a height advantage, so he will be forced to suggest that you both go and sit somewhere more comfortable.

You will have won the non-verbal proxemic battle, and unless he is sufficiently confident to risk an open verbal clash ('Would you mind very much taking yourself off my desk, you're sitting on some rather important confidential papers I'm preparing for the chairman') the best he can now hope for is to establish equality.

Seating arrangements are another revealing aspect of proxemic behaviour. For example, whereas academics tend to sit sideways on to their office doors and are comparatively easy-going in their use of personal space zones, businessmen and civil servants characteristically sit facing their doors. This is because academics spend much of their time talking informally with students or colleagues, while businessmen and civil servants have to conduct their affairs in a more formal way, and may often need to impress their visitors. The distance regarded as comfortable for conversation when standing tends to be doubled when people are sitting down. This may be affected both by the size of the room and by the sex of the people involved: the larger the room, the closer two people will sit when they are its only occupants (though a small minority of people choose to sit very much *further* apart in a large room), and women tend to sit closer together than men. There are also national differences in the position favoured by two people sharing a small table: Englishmen and Americans like to sit at 90 degrees to each other (in a pub they prefer to sit side by side with their backs to the wall), while Arabs and Swedes prefer to face one another.

Our demands for personal space and privacy are most easily

understood as a request that other people should acknowledge our existence and importance, and allow us space we can call our own (personal space) and time and a place to be alone (privacy). Privacy may be defined as *chosen* separateness, to distinguish it from isolation or loneliness, and it represents an attempt to free oneself from the power or influence of other people. In most societies, conventional morality recognises that certain activities are most appropriately carried out in private – copulation and defecation, for example. These are not universal norms, because there are variations both between cultures and, over time, within a culture. There are still societies in which children are allowed to watch adults (other than their own mothers) copulating; and it is not so very long ago that the introduction of a new fiscal measure known as income tax in our own society was denounced as the most outrageous invasion of privacy. But most of us need a certain amount of privacy, and it probably has the function of helping to maintain our sense of personal identity. Therefore institutions that seek to foster team-spirit at the expense of individuality deliberately restrict access to privacy. This is most marked in the armed forces and boarding schools – I was never totally convinced by the explanation given at my old school, a very traditional, character-building establishment, that the provision of lavatories without doors was just a relic of a nineteenth-century economy drive.

Negotiations and intrusions

I have implied that our territorial and social instincts are opposed to each other, but, in at least one respect, territoriality can also contribute to the smooth running of an intimate relationship. When two people decide to live together, they soon reach agreement about where each of them will keep their clothes, who will sleep on which side of the bed, which chair belongs to whom, and so on. Without such territorial arrangements, the relationship would be threatened by an endless series of disputes. Because these arrangements imply a degree of permanency which might jeopardise the success of a relationship between a pair of free-wheeling, independent spirits, we would expect to find differences in territorial behaviour between cohabiting couples who are married and those who are not. This is exactly what was found in a recent study of American students living together. Territorial agreements such as those described above were found to be significantly less marked amongst unmarried cohabiting couples, and – unlike married couples – they tended to reserve areas in the house where either could be alone, with a guarantee of privacy. It was also found that when a couple who had been living together for some time decided to get married, they remained significantly less territorial in their living arrangements than the average married couple, but surrendered their private areas.

This study has interesting implications for 'trial' marriages. Living together may allow you to get to know each other well before committing yourselves formally, but it is an inadequate preparation for the restriction of individual privacy which marriage seems to impose.

We are willing to accept limitations on our privacy as part of the price we must pay for the pleasures of an intimate relationship, and we have already seen that intimates – whether married to us or not – have the right to penetrate even the innermost zone of our personal space. But what happens when our personal space is violated without authorisation, or when other attacks are made on what remains of our territorial instinct?

We saw earlier that our reaction to unavoidable violations of personal space – for example, during the rush hour – is to pretend that the invader isn't there: we declare him a non-person. But even when the violation is deliberate, the evidence suggests that our inclination is either to ignore it or to respond by taking ourselves elsewhere, rather than to fight for our territorial rights. There have been many experiments which make this point. In one, a female experimenter came and sat close to solitary female readers who were working in a library. Tables in the library had eight chairs, and newcomers to the library would normally seat themselves either at an empty table or, if all the tables were occupied, at an occupied table, but as far as possible away from the other occupant(s). The solitary readers were visibly disturbed by the experimenter's deviant behaviour, and a majority had moved elsewhere within fifteen minutes of her arrival, especially if she had not merely taken an adjacent chair but moved it as close as she could to the unwitting subject without actually making physical contact. It is not certain what made the subjects move away: was it because they felt their identity or status was being attacked, or did they fear a homosexual advance, or just feel uneasy in the presence of someone who was behaving so oddly? Whatever the reason, it is clear that we find spatial invasions disturbing.

Perhaps the most surprising aspect of this and similar experiments is how rarely we try to counter-attack – only one of the eighty subjects who were harassed in the library asked the invader to move over or to make more room. In a second experiment in which intruders sat down at meal tables clearly reserved for – and partially occupied by – groups to which they did not belong, by far the most common reaction of the rightful occupants (of both sexes) was to ignore the invasion completely. So although we may have a highly developed sense of our spatial and territorial requirements and rights, we have become so thoroughly socialised that we ignore or walk away from situations in which they are obviously infringed. The pursuit of peaceful coexistence seems to be a more potent force in human behaviour than the defence of territory, which supports the view that we have come much closer to abandoning our territorial inheritance than the ethologists would have us believe.

2 Living
with our surroundings

We shape our dwellings, and afterwards our dwellings shape us
Winston Churchill

What effect do your physical surroundings really have on the quality of life you enjoy? I believe that social scientists and planners are at fault in attributing an assortment of social evils – mental illness, broken families, crime and violence, for example – to the effects of overcrowded living conditions, and to certain distinctive features of modern urban architecture such as high-rise blocks of flats. I suspect that the role which the physical environment plays in shaping our lives has been seriously over-estimated, and that a number of widely held beliefs about the force of architectural determinism – the view that our lives are shaped by our surroundings – are myths.

The madding crowd
Probably the most influential of these beliefs concerns the effects of overcrowding, and this is a further example of the danger of using the results of animal studies to interpret human behaviour. Much attention has been given to the work of John Calhoun, who observed what happens when colonies of rats are provided with all the food and water they need, and left to get on with their lives in an enclosed area. A colony might be started with four male and six female rats (male rats like to gather a harem), for whom there is ample space, and it grows rapidly until there is a vast number of rats in the cage. At a certain point, however, the population stops growing and begins to decline, slowly at first but then quite rapidly. There are even indications that the colony would die out altogether, though I know of no experiment which has gone on long enough to test this.

What has excited people about these studies is the striking

change in behaviour which accompanies the increase in population density. There is a huge increase in infant mortality, largely due to a breakdown in maternal skills. So far as the males are concerned, a very small number of the toughest manage to preserve the comfortable and productive 'normal' lifestyle of the rat, collecting a harem and protecting their nest and family, thereby adding to the population of the colony. But as the population increases, a growing number of males finds it impossible to sustain this pattern of living, and instead adopts either an asocial or, more commonly, an antisocial way of life. Some become recluses, avoiding all social or sexual contact with the rest of the colony; they remain sleek and well-groomed (Calhoun calls them 'beautiful ones'), but their survival is essentially an unproductive business. The rest of the males, and some females, settle for a lifestyle which is not merely unproductive, but actually counter-productive. The stronger males become 'marauders', launching pointless attacks on other rats, and forcing their sexual attentions on anything that moves, regardless of age or sex. The weaker males and some females gather in large groups (Calhoun calls them 'probers'), milling about and fighting savagely amongst themselves. In these circumstances, it is hardly surprising that the population of the colony declines dramatically. Although only the beautiful ones actually abandon sex altogether, the products of the frenetic sexual activity of the marauders and the homeless probers have little chance of survival.

High density is also found to have at least one significant effect on the rats' physiology: those living in crowded conditions develop bigger adrenal glands, a sign that they are producing more adrenalin. Since the production of adrenalin is part of the body's response to stress, we may assume that high population density is a stressor. However, it is not the cramped living quarters *per se* which cause stress, because the actual amount of space available to an individual is found to be irrelevant to the size of its adrenal glands. Ten rats in a nine square foot cage develop larger adrenals than a solitary rat in a one by one foot cage, although there is little difference in the amount of space per rat in the two cages. What is more, you can increase the size of the ten rats' cage by more than thirty times, so that each of

20

the ten has considerably more space than the solitary rat, but the ten are still found to have larger adrenal glands than the one.

This suggests that the dramatic effects of high population density may not after all be a result of the restricted space available. Instead, it seems to be the close presence of a large number of other animals which is stressful. This is a blow for the doctrine of architectural determinism, because it belittles the importance of an animal's *physical* surroundings, and suggests that his social life – especially the number of animals with which he has to interact – has a much greater influence on his well-being. If this is the case, it is unlikely that we can learn much about the effects of overcrowding on humans from these experiments, because human beings have at their disposal a range of social skills for controlling and limiting the intensity of their social relations, even in the most crowded conditions, that are not available to rats.

We saw earlier that people respond to a stressful social encounter simply by walking away from it. When someone comes and sits too close to you in a library, you go and sit somewhere else. If the house seems to be full of screaming children, you suddenly remember that you need to go out and buy some cigarettes. And if life in the city becomes too much for you, you can either recuperate with a weekend out of town or take the more drastic step of going to live somewhere more tranquil. Left to their own devices animals too emigrate from an area which has become overcrowded, but in the experiments we have been discussing they are denied this opportunity.

Unfortunately this fact has been ignored by many social scientists, who have used Calhoun's rat-colonies to explain what goes on in our inner-city slums. Deep significance has been attached to the parallel between slum landlords and racketeers on the one hand, and the dominant rats on the other. Calhoun's reclusive 'beautiful ones' have been likened to hippies and beatniks (though neither of these groups was famous for its lack of interest in sex), while the antisocial activities of juvenile street-gangs and criminal psychopaths has been represented as equivalent to that of the 'probers' and 'marauders' in the rat colony. The socially undesirable behaviour of all those groups has been laid at the door of the cramped conditions in inner cities, with anxiety, suicide, schizophrenia and divorce thrown in for good measure. As a scenario, it has a pleasing simplicity and only one fault: there is no evidence whatever that high population density itself leads to any of these social evils.

Is overcrowding bad for us?
So far as crime is concerned, the crime rate in cities may be higher than in less densely populated areas of a country (though remember that the level of criminal activity has rocketed in recent years, while cities have actually been *losing* population), but analysis of the statistics reveals no connection between the population density of a given neighbourhood and its crime rate. When areas within a city are equated for income, crowded neighbourhoods produce no more crime than those which are less populous. In fact, in poorer areas, there seems to be *less* crime in neighbourhoods with the densest population. The reason why it is popularly believed that overcrowding leads to crime is that the poor get caught committing more crimes than the rich, and poor people tend to live in more densely populated neighbourhoods than the rich. But it is a fairly simple statistical matter to remove the effects of income and educational level from the equation that population density equals crime, and when you do so the equation collapses. Moreover, neighbourhoods of cities in which the houses are built very close to each other or where there are a large number of high-rise blocks of flats, do *not* have a higher crime rate than areas in which the houses are built further apart and there are fewer high-rises. Nor do areas with a preponderance of houses and flats which offer little space to their occupants have more crime than those which provide more luxurious and spacious accommodation.

There is no convincing evidence either that crowding leads to any other form of mental, physical or social pathology. Once you allow for the fact that people of certain ethnic origins and certain income levels tend to live in neighbourhoods with particular population densities, the statistics show no connection between population density (measured either by the number of people per acre or by the average size of their living quarters) and mental illness, infant mortality, venereal disease or any of the other social ills which are supposed to result from overcrowding. Most of the empirical studies on which I base this claim have been carried out in North America, but their results have been confirmed elsewhere. The authors of a recent report in New Zealand went so far as to turn the conventional wisdom on its head: noticing that population density was actually *negatively* related to the number of prescriptions issued for tranquillisers and anti-depressant drugs, they proposed that loneliness might be a greater source of stress than overcrowding. This suggestion is supported by statistics from America which show that the incidence of peptic ulcers, insomnia and high blood-pressure, which are all thought to be related to stress, is actually higher in rural than in urban areas. People who live in cities are more prone to contagious diseases and traffic accidents, but these are due to increased contact with other people and to congested roads rather than to the actual number of people per building. Surveys of people's attitudes to life and their subjective feelings of well-being paint a similar picture: city dwellers are if anything *more* satisfied with their lives than their country cousins, though this difference only holds up in certain parts of the world. In America, people living in communities with less than 2500 inhabitants are found to be significantly less satisfied with their lives than those living in towns with between 2500 and 5000 residents. When a conurbation tops the million mark, its inhabitants start to express more dissatisfaction with their lives, but they remain more satisfied than people living in rural communities.

However, old beliefs die hard, and architectural determinists are not beaten yet. Research staff at the Home Office in London failed to find any connection between the design of blocks of flats and their crime rates in another recent study (they had anticipated that the number of doors or staircases in a building might affect the vandalism rate). But instead of concluding that no such relationship existed, they merely suggested that the architecture–crime link must be a very complex one! A more plausible general principle would seem to be that buildings are less important than the characteristics – including the social skills – of the people who live in them.

But what happens when we look at crowding on a smaller

23

scale? Surely the more people there are in a room, the more uneasy we feel and the less competently we do our jobs. And when a large number of people are crammed together in a small room, don't they start behaving more aggressively? Well, you might think so (I certainly did until I started looking at the evidence), but laboratory studies suggest otherwise. Because of its importance for the space programme – astronauts have to live and work together in a tiny area for long periods of time, in circumstances in which errors may well prove fatal – the question has been thoroughly investigated, and once again there is no conclusive evidence either that crowding *per se* is unpleasant or that it has an adverse effect on behaviour. In fact, when two or three astronauts are confined together for up to twenty days they are found to get along better in a small area (70 cubic feet per person) than in a larger area (200 cubic feet).

Of course the sort of people who volunteer to become astronauts are hardly typical members of the population: they are highly motivated to overcome any adverse effects which over-crowding might have, so it would be rash to make too much of this finding. But other experimenters have confined groups of students and housewives in rooms of various sizes (admittedly for much shorter periods of time), and they have found that room-size has no effect whatever on the subjects' performance of a wide variety of intellectual tasks. Nor is there any evidence that crowding, as distinct from smell, heat, fear or physical discomfort, is experienced as stressful. So far as aggression is concerned, the position is complicated by an intriguing sex difference. In experiments in which both men and women took part, the size of the room in which they were confined had no *overall* effect on the incidence of aggression, as measured either by the amount of competitive play when subjects were required to take part in a game in which they could adopt either a competitive or a cooperative strategy, or by the severity of 'sentences' meted out when they were required to act out the role of a trial jury. Men did tend to become more aggressive when crowded, but women actually became *less* aggressive.

At last we have some evidence that crowding may affect behaviour, though not necessarily for the worse. Since there is very strong empirical evidence that men are typically more

24

aggressive creatures than women (this is not a male chauvinist remark, but the considered judgement of psychologists such as Eleanor Maccoby and Carol Jacklin, who have reviewed all the research in this area in *The Psychology of Sex Differences*), perhaps the effect of crowding is simply to *intensify* whatever reaction we would have to a situation in less crowded circumstances. When we are doing something we feel neutral about, crowding is unlikely to affect us one way or the other. But when we are doing something we feel strongly about – whether we like or dislike it – crowding can heighten our feelings. At a party, the more the merrier; when we have an important interview, the fewer people on the interviewing panel the less frightened we feel. But the fact remains that crowding itself is not *causing* us to feel anything. It is not a *primary* influence on our behaviour: it merely intensifies feelings and reactions which already exist for quite different reasons.

Big is beautiful

Let me expose another fallacy which reflects the common belief that cities have an adverse effect on those who live in them. Cities are attacked for being not only overcrowded but also impersonal, numbing their inhabitants' responsiveness to the needs of their fellow-men. Country folk, by contrast, being free from the dehumanising and debilitating pressures of urban living, are held to be paragons of virtue, who regard a day as wasted if it passes without giving them the opportunity to offer assistance to a stranger in need. Alas, this idyllic picture is somewhat marred by the results of a recent experiment. Students at the University of Hawaii, from rural and urban backgrounds, were shown into rooms in the laboratory where they were asked to complete a standard psychological test. As they were working, a stooge knocked at the door of the room, saying 'Tom, Tom, are you there?' He then came in and tripped, dropping a brick and moaning 'Oh, my foot!' The students who had been brought up in rural communities, far from leaping to the rescue, actually turned out to be *less* likely to offer assistance than their urban counterparts. It would be rash to attach too much importance to the results of a single study, and we know that there are differences between cities in

25

the response which a stranger can expect to a plea for assistance. Another study has shown that whereas Athenians are more likely to help a foreigner than a fellow-Greek, the natives of Boston and Paris, though prepared to assist a compatriot, tend to be unhelpful if not actually misleading when a foreigner asks them for directions. We are all familiar with these regional variations, but many studies support the conclusions of the Hawaiian experiment, that city-dwellers are *not* generally less helpful than people who live in the country.

I make no apology if I sound like a public-relations man for the Defence of Cities League, for I believe that the anti-urban living, let's-all-get-back-to-the-soil movement reflects a fundamental misunderstanding of human nature and a repudiation of evolutionary progress. It also ignores the fact that we are not going to stop living in cities (nor should we), and it has given politicians and planners an excuse to allow our cities to become very much less agreeable places to live in. I suspect that things start going wrong in cities not when too many people are gathered together, but when there are too few. The way to reduce crime in the streets and parks of a city is to ensure that they are full of people, and the best way to protect an apartment block from the attention of vandals and thieves is to provide it with shared public areas and facilities which encourage people to meet and get to know each other.

It could be argued that urban living represents the highest rather than the lowest mode of human life, because only large cities are able to support a really diverse mixture of specialist skills, crafts and talents: it is in cities that you find the highest expression of the culture which sets us apart from other animals.

You and your surroundings

Although I have attacked some extreme manifestations of the doctrine of architectural determinism, I certainly don't mean to imply that we are wholly indifferent to or unaffected by our physical surroundings. Researchers in the new discipline of environmental psychology have confirmed that we carry in our heads maps of our surroundings which are significantly different from a geographer's map of the same area, and that we find our way about cities by using a series of personal landmarks. These mental maps not only enable us to function efficiently, but also offer emotional security – we become anxious when we get lost. Our distress when a familiar landmark is pulled down is not just a sign of sentimentality, but a reminder that stress has been defined as anything which forces us to adapt or change. Both moving house and living in an area which is redeveloped can be stressful experiences, so it is not surprising to find that moving house increases the risk of a person becoming clinically depressed or even committing suicide. These findings have important implications for the practice of urban redevelopment. First, it seems desirable to identify – by canvassing local opinion – the psychologically important landmarks in the area which is to be redeveloped: architectural merit ought not to be the only reason for deciding to preserve a building. Secondly, too much uniformity in urban architecture should be avoided, not merely on the grounds that it is boring, but also because it makes it more difficult to form a mental map of the area.

There is a clear pattern to the way in which our mental maps distort geographical reality. For example, we tend to underestimate distances when they are in the direction of the city centre, which may explain why people often use shops which are towards the city centre even though those in the opposite direction may actually be nearer. Some cities are easier to form a mental map of than others, and in these *legible* cities (Los Angeles and Glasgow are examples), people are found to underestimate the distance between points, while in cities which are harder to visualise, such as Tokyo, there is a tendency to overestimate distances. The legibility of a city is therefore likely to affect both the mobility and social life of its inhabitants. There is also evidence that our image of a city is greatly influenced by the particular form of transport we most often use to travel around it: for example, studies have shown that London seems much smaller to regular tube travellers than to bus-users. This may explain why it is so difficult to get commuters to leave their cars at home: change to another form of transport may save the commuter time and money, but it also forces him to make radical changes in his concept of the city.

27

People have a personal concept not only of their city but also of their neighbourhood. When shown a map of the area surrounding their house and asked to draw a line around what they thought to be their neighbourhood, three-quarters of the housewives who took part in a survey in Cambridge delineated an area of – on average – 100 acres. The size of what they regarded as their neighbourhood was not affected by its population density or by whether or not they owned a car. However, it is not certain how potent an influence on people's lives their sense of belonging to a neighbourhood is. Often it takes a threat from outside to remind people of its existence – nothing brings a neighbourhood together faster than the rumour that a motorway is going to be driven through the middle of it.

The importance of the neighbourhood in normal circumstances may be in question, but no such doubts exist about the importance of our home. Every other Saturday I take great pleasure in watching my local football team make mincemeat of most, if not all, comers on their home ground. But on the rare occasions when I venture further afield to watch them playing away from home, I find it hard to believe that I am looking at the same players. At home, all is aggression and confident skill; four miles away across London, they are transformed into timid bunglers. Unfortunately, I can offer little hope to football managers who are scratching their heads to find a solution to this problem. The home-team advantage seems to be a phenomenon with unmistakable biological antecedents, and another reminder that we are not yet free from our territorial inheritance. In case you are ever tempted to bet on the result of a fight between two fish, ethologists' observations suggest that your money would be safer on the fish that is on home territory, irrespective of its size. Similarly, when two monkeys have a confrontation, the advantage enjoyed by whichever is higher in the pack's hierarchy is at least partially offset by home advantage. Despite the dangers of moving too swiftly from the observation of animals to the interpretation of human behaviour, it is difficult to resist drawing an analogy between these findings and the upsets which often occur when a modest team takes on – at home – one of the giants of the Football League.

28

Footballers are not alone in their atavistic behaviour. For all of us, our homes remain the one place where we are permitted to indulge our territorial instincts. We are still subject to constraints, but most 'free' societies allow people considerable latitude as to how they behave in their homes. The law recognises our right to choose whom we allow to enter our house, and takes a relatively tolerant view when we use methods to eject uninvited visitors which would be frowned on in other circumstances. Nor is there any reason to suppose that our homes are becoming less important to us. Although the traditional nuclear-family unit is weakening as children move away from the parental home at an earlier age, some sociologists consider that the most significant change in social habits over the last century has been the growth of *homeliness* (including house-pride) at the expense of community life.

Psychologists are interested both in how people are affected by the homes in which they live and in what they do to their homes, because it is clear that the interaction between people and their houses is a two-way process. Psychoanalysts have described houses as symbols of the mother's body, and proposed that the confidence with which a child learns to move away from his mother will determine how severely he will be affected by moving house as an adult. This may sound rather far-fetched, but it is clear that the physical features of houses do affect both the children and adults who live in them. John and Elizabeth Newson, in their extensive investigation of the way in which English children are brought up, have shown that larger houses – especially those with gardens – allow middle-class parents to play a much more active supervisory role in the life of their pre-school children than working-class parents. Thus architecture can affect the quality of socialisation, and help to preserve middle-class values. The introduction of the electric light bulb and central heating systems has had the effect of dispersing a family about the house, and this may have loosened the traditional structure of the family unit. Equally important, the replacement of the cold and miserable outside-privy with the warm and comfortable inside-lavatory may have made toilet training a less traumatic business. If Freud is right, this ought to be increasing the number of people with generous, outgoing personalities, and one environmental psychologist has gone so far as to suggest that 'flush toilets in warm interiors may actually be bringing us a tiny step closer to international harmony' – architectural determinism run riot!

Given the importance of our houses, it is not surprising to find that we have pretty definite ideas about how individual rooms should look. We arrange the furniture to suit different purposes (the intending seducer places the sofa in a dimly-lit corner rather than in the centre of the room), and there is general agreement about what features make a room 'friendly' or pleasant to sit in. Studies in which people are asked to comment on both actual rooms and pictures of rooms with certain features altered, show that we remain loyal to traditional stereotypes in this respect. A room with a sloping roof and a good-sized window is judged to be more friendly, while we still look upon two armchairs facing a fireplace as the best ambience in which to read or chat. We are also surprisingly consistent in our feeling about how large our main living rooms should be: bedrooms and kitchens may have shrunk and expanded with changes in the economic climate, but the typical English living room has remained a constant 150 to 200 square feet in size since the end of the 1914–1918 war.

What is surprising is the discrepancy between our ideas and those of the architects who design our houses. In a recent empirical study, less than half of the architects questioned were able to guess either where the sofa would be placed in the living rooms of a council housing-estate (they actually tended to be placed across the back of the room), or the correct location of the TV (generally, in the right-hand corner facing the fireplace). The architects also tended to divide their 'ideal' living room into different activity zones, and to keep an area free for circulation, although the tenants adopted neither practice. This may just have reflected a difference in the way in which architects and Cardiff council-tenants like to organise their lives, but no such explanation can be given for the finding that the current British Standard for the height of a sink is suitable only for women of less than average height. This is a clear instance of sloppy design, and it is just one example of the way in which ergonomists and environmental psychologists are beginning to force designers and architects to acknowledge that buildings should answer the demands of their users rather than some abstract aesthetic principle. However, there is still a long way to go in convincing architects that buildings are primarily places in which people live and work: of the forty-five criteria used in awarding prizes for architecture, only two relate to the extent to which a building fulfils human needs.

3 Eating

If you were asked why you ate, and were willing to answer what sounds like a pretty simple-minded question, you might reply: to stay alive (in the long term), or because I get hungry (in the short term). At least one of these answers is incorrect, but they are sensible replies, because eating does of course have survival value – if we stop eating, we die – and it is to some extent under physiological control. All successful species are able to regulate how much they eat according to how much energy they expend, and most manage to maintain a constant body-weight over long periods of time without the aid of a weighing machine. We don't have to learn to eat, as we have to learn some of the skills and habits discussed in later chapters, because we are born with a small repertoire of behaviour – reflexes – which includes the ability to suck as well as a tendency to attach our mouths to any promising-looking source of nutrition which appears in our field of vision.

We are, if you like, genetically programmed to eat. What is more we seem to have a natural ability to eat the right things. This was demonstrated in an experiment of classical simplicity – if, to contemporary eyes, doubtful propriety – carried out in an American orphanage in the 1930s. Over a period of six years, children from the age of weaning upwards were confronted at mealtimes with a large range of foods placed in separate dishes, and allowed to eat whatever they liked. Staff at the orphanage were forbidden to direct their choices in any way, and so far as the experimenters could tell these instructions were obeyed. The staff stood behind the dishes and fed the children if necessary, but only after a child had pointed at a particular dish. To adult eyes, the meals were prolonged and messy affairs, and some of the choices of menu were bizarre – for example, liver was a popular breakfast choice. But the children were astonishingly good at selecting a balanced diet containing the appropriate number of calories, and indeed enjoyed conspicuously good health. Some of the children had rickets when they entered the institution, but they soon found cod-liver oil among the dishes and drank it until they had cured themselves, whereupon they gave it up. Moreover, the staff could always tell in advance when a child was about to become ill because he would stop eating the day before. When he started eating again, they knew he would be well the next day. We have to be slightly careful when interpreting these findings, because of the range of dishes on offer. All the food was natural and unprocessed – meat, fish, vegetables, milk, water, sea-salt, and so forth. They were not offered bread and jam, tea or sugar, or sweets. When rats are used in this sort of 'cafeteria' experiment, they sometimes give up eating altogether in favour of a sucrose solution, when this is on the menu, and we can't be certain that the children in the orphanage would have chosen such an exemplary diet had they been offered the temptation of food containing sugar. Nevertheless, it is clear that eating is under fine biological control, so it seems sensible to begin by looking at the way in which our brains and bodies control the habit.

Physiological needs

There is clearly more to eating than meets the eye – or the mouth. Some years ago it was suggested that there is a *primary feeding centre* in the brain which causes us to eat, and a *satiation centre* which, by inhibiting the activity of the primary eating centre when we have had enough, causes us to stop eating. Experiments show that rats continue to eat and stay in good health even when they have been operated on so that food is delivered directly to the stomach instead of being taken in through the mouth, which seems to imply that eating is largely under the control of the brain, and that we need not bother too much about the role of sensory cues provided by taste or smell. However it has become clear that this view, which dominated the study of eating for twenty years, is too simple. Recent experiments have shown that the amount we eat at a meal is determined both by the taste of food in our mouths and also by what we see on our plates. In one experiment, people were given a drink immediately before a sandwich lunch. For half of those taking part the starch content of the drink was 65 per cent, for the others only 5 per cent. Everyone finished his meal with a yoghurt which had one of two distinctive flavours, depending upon the level of starch in his pre-lunch drink. As you might expect, all subjects started by eating the same number of sandwiches whatever the starch content of their pre-meal drink, but they very soon began to eat more after the dilute than the concentrated starch. What is surprising is that when the experimenters then served identical 35 per cent starch drinks to everybody, the amount a person ate still seemed to be determined by the type of yoghurt he could see on his tray.

Food preferences and fads are of course quite familiar, and they are rarely based on anything so rational as carbohydrate levels. A recent study found that boys between the ages of nine and fifteen have a sweeter tooth than girls, and that food preferences are not genetically determined. Identical twins showed very little similarity in their preferences, a surprising finding since they are not only genetically indentical but also very likely to have been exposed to similar diets. Perhaps their strong need to be unique encourages the development of different tastes.

As well as establishing the importance of the mouth in normal eating (and even more so in abnormal eating, as we shall see later), recent research has indicated that the liver rather than the brain may be the most important stimulus for the sensation of hunger. The liver is best placed to integrate information about calorie levels at any given moment, and it seems likely that the hunger centres in the brain are triggered by a message from the liver that it is no longer receiving sufficient supplies of energy from the intestines or from the fat reserves to maintain essential bodily functions.

Creatures of habit

But there is a lot more to eating than hunger. Consider what happens when you sit down to a meal prepared by a really bad cook: your hunger may vanish as the first forkful reaches your mouth, but unless you are either socially gauche or exceptionally self-confident you will not stop eating. In fact, if you are rich enough to buy books, it is very unlikely that you ever eat primarily because you are hungry. You probably eat far in excess of your actual biological need, and never experience more than the mildest pangs of hunger. So your second answer to my original question – why do you eat? – ought perhaps to be revised: you eat in order to avoid hunger (both general and for specific substances) rather than because you *are* hungry. Western man doesn't believe in eating on an empty stomach. But this is still grossly deficient as an explanation of your presence at the table at mealtimes. The word 'mealtimes' offers a clue – much eating behaviour, especially if it is part of the traditional British pattern of four meals a day, can be explained by the time of day. You eat because it is one o'clock, regardless of whether or not you actually feel hungry. Of course it may also be five hours since you last ate. But delaying one meal has little effect on the amount which is eaten at the next, and this suggests that habit plays a much larger part in determining our eating than the immediate demands of the body.

The pattern of daily life tends to be organised around meals, though the actual details of the pattern established vary both between cultures and between individuals in the same culture, depending on circumstances. For example, a woman's day may change drastically if she stops being a mother and goes back to work; but she will continue to locate events by referring to meals – lunchtime, after tea, and so on.

Meals of course have other functions than merely eating. You may take a lunch-*break* or have a *working* lunch – either will affect the way you feel. There is evidence that eating lunch has a tranquillising effect: people describe themselves as less anxious and depressed after lunch than before. But it may have less desirable effects as well, for it has been shown that although eating lunch helps to protect you from the over-arousing effects of working in a very noisy environment, it may also increase the risk of accidents by reducing your concentration. There is a period in the early afternoon when we function less efficiently than our best, known as the 'post-lunch dip', which suggests that the practice of taking a nap or siesta after lunch is based on sound biological principles.

Meals are highly structured and conventionalised affairs. A recent sociological investigation of British eating habits found complete agreement in different parts of the country as to what the day's meals should consist of, as well as very rigid rules about the order in which dishes should appear. You may consider yourself a pretty bohemian character, but you would still baulk at eating dessert before the main course. Over the centuries there have been considerable changes in eating habits: the unbridled gluttony of the Middle Ages gave way in the eighteenth century to an ascetic condemnation of all sauces and seasoning, and this in turn was somewhat softened as modern notions about cooking were established in the last century. But in the shorter term, it is surprising how little our eating habits have been changed by the introduction of new techniques for preserving and marketing food. It remains to be seen whether the threatened global shortage of natural foodstuffs will radically alter what we eat.

Social psychologists have been struck by the extent to which our behaviour at the table is governed by rules. Convention dictates both seating arrangements and the order in which people are served. The implements we use for transferring food from plate to mouth must be chosen (particularly when the meal is a formal affair) according to conventions which entirely ignore the fact that cutlery is objectively interchangeable. Who has not looked with longing at a spoon while attempting to eat peas with a fork slavishly held the 'right' way up? The power of this particular flummery can be gauged from the stranglehold it exerts even on people who seem to be relatively free from conventional inhibitions. Norman Mailer makes the point nicely in his novel *An American Dream*, where a character is less upset by having to admit to murdering his wife than by being caught using the wrong fork.

Meals also have a celebratory function. We celebrate Christmas with a goose or a turkey, birthdays and weddings with a cake. Roast food is universally recognised as appropriate for celebrations, while boiling is left for everyday preparation. Food is the subject of many religious taboos which impose dietary restrictions, and temporary selective abstinence is commonly used to mark either a specific day (Yom Kippur, for example) or a longer period of religious significance (Ramadan or Lent).

Mealtimes have other social uses (that they *are* primarily social affairs can be seen from the stigma attached to eating alone, and the fact that people forced to do so will often read a book or newspaper, a practice normally frowned upon at all meals other than breakfast): for adults, they provide an opportunity for informal social encounters, free from the burden of the day's tasks. And no one would think of giving a party without food or drink. For children, however, meals are events of even greater significance.

Children and food

Throughout childhood, meals play a crucial role in socialisation – the process whereby children adapt themselves to society as they learn how things (and people) are. During the first year of life, feeding time is by far the child's most important social occasion. What happens at these times hugely affects his view of the world and – particularly – of its other inhabitants. It will certainly influence the course of his socialisation, and may partially determine what sort of person he becomes, although the long-term effects of very early experience are still a matter of dispute among psychologists. According to Freud, the importance of what happens when a child eats diminishes after the first year as the emphasis of socialisation switches to other areas such as toilet training. But the relationship between eating, growing and a child's happiness is well established, and best summed up in the words of the Bible: 'Better a dinner of herbs where love is than a stalled ox and hatred therewith'.

On the other hand, eating can be a major source of conflict, as any parent knows. The meal table becomes a battleground, as children seek to win the struggle of wills and manipulate their parents by refusing food or developing unpredictable fads. Parents worry that the children are not being properly fed and, in order to persuade them to eat, become more likely to give in over other matters. But the child's behaviour is revealed to be a ploy, because he eats perfectly well at school or when out to tea at someone else's house. Children realise that home is the place where parents try to impose their authority, so they keep their powder dry for the skirmishes that matter, content meanwhile to fill their stomachs elsewhere.

We should also remember that children's views about food are rather different from those of adults, who rarely have to eat food they don't like. Studies of primary schoolchildren in the playground have shown that they draw a distinction between food for meals and food to be eaten between meals. This is a distinction many adults would recognise, but in terms rather different from those children use. To a child, meals consist of things like sausages, cabbage, jelly and ice-cream, which are often treated as objects of humour because of their shape, messiness and so on: they feature largely in his vocabulary of abuse. Food which is eaten between meals – sweets and fruit, for example – is regarded in a more favourable light, and is used in the playground as a token of friendship or as an object for swapping and bargaining.

Too much of a good thing

I said earlier that eating is something we are naturally good at. Certainly the orphanage children were remarkably accomplished at eating what they needed to remain healthy and grow normally. I also suggested that we rarely eat because we are hungry. But what about people who eat too much or too little for the good of their health?

On the basis of their experience as actuaries, the Metropolitan Life Insurance Company of America have published a table which shows the maximum desirable weight for men and women of all heights. Above these levels the rate of mortality rises sharply, and people whose weight is more than 20 per cent above the maximum desirable are classified as *obese*. The prevalence of obesity is astonishingly high. One survey in London found that over a third of the men and nearly half the women sampled were clinically obese. It is not therefore surprising that at any given time 10 per cent of the British population is actively trying to lose weight, or that each year more than a third of us go on a diet. Obesity is not a peculiarly British disease, being widespread throughout the developed world, but it is unequally distributed. It is more common in women than in men, and it is also more frequent among the old than the young. At least in industrialised countries, it is more prevalent among the lower than the higher social classes, presumably because diets rich in carbohydrate which are associated with being overweight are cheaper than those containing proportionally more protein.

Maximum desirable weights

(The figures in brackets denote 20 per cent above the desirable weight. Height is shown in feet and inches, weight in stones and pounds.)

Height	Female	Male
4 10	8 7 (10 3)	
11	8 10 (10 6)	
5 0	8 13 (10 10)	
1	9 2 (11 0)	
2	9 5 (11 3)	10 1 (12 1)
3	9 8 (11 6)	10 4 (12 5)
4	9 12 (11 12)	10 8 (12 10)
5	10 2 (12 2)	10 12 (13 1)
6	10 6 (12 7)	11 2 (13 6)
7	10 10 (12 12)	11 7 (13 11)
8	11 0 (13 3)	11 12 (14 3)
9	11 4 (13 8)	12 2 (14 8)
10	11 9 (14 0)	12 6 (14 13)
11	12 0 (14 6)	12 11 (15 5)
6 0	12 5 (14 12)	13 2 (15 11)
1		13 7 (16 3)
2		13 12 (16 9)
3		14 3 (17 1)

(Derived from the statistical bulletin of the Metropolitan Life Insurance Company (1969) *40*: 1–4.)

The immediate cause of obesity is clear: you get fat if you eat more than enough to replenish the energy you have used up. What is less clear is why some people get fat while others don't. There are three different sorts of obesity, which can be distinguished by the age at which and the circumstances in which the condition appears for the first time, and two of them seem to be precipitated by separate physiological causes. One sort of obesity is associated with abnormalities in either the number or the size of a person's fat cells or adipocytes. The *number* of fat cells you have is fixed very early in life, probably by the end of the first year, by genes and your early feeding experience. Breast-fed babies are known to be less prone subsequently to obesity than those fed on the bottle, perhaps because the changes which occur in the composition of human milk during the course of a feed serve as a cue to the baby to stop feeding. The uniform flavour of powdered milk provides no such cues for the bottle-fed baby to regulate his intake. He therefore takes more nourishment and increases both the number of his fat cells and his later food requirement. Overfeeding in infancy may result in *hyperplastic obesity*, which is characterised by an abnormally high number of adipocytes and an apparent need for high-calorie intake. This type of obesity may also be caused by *under*nourishment of the child's mother during the early (though not the later) stages of pregnancy.

So it seems that the number of fat cells each person has is fixed at a characteristic level by heredity and early feeding. This level is then apparently preserved by the activity of the feeding centres in the brain mentioned earlier. If it is high, the individual is programmed to be obese, and enforced weight reduction will produce an energy deficit similar to starvation. It is hardly surprising that this type of obesity is so hard to reverse.

By eating too much consistently over the years we may increase the *size* of our fat cells; this also increases our demand for food and may result in a second condition, called *hypertrophic obesity*, which does not appear until after maturity. The normal weight-regulation mechanism is astonishingly finely balanced. Dieticians claim that if a normal-weight twenty-year-old eats just one slice of bread and butter each day in excess of his calorie requirements, in ten years time he will be nearly eight stone overweight! Hypertrophic obesity is however easier to halt, by reversing the eating habits which cause it. The third, less serious, condition is *reactive obesity*, which usually occurs for the first time later in life as a response to such stressful circumstances as bereavement or the menopause.

40

Food is a solace and a comfort, so there is no need to seek out some deep-rooted pathological cause to explain why we turn to it in times of stress.

Do obese people have anything in common, apart from their fatness? Stanley Schachter, a leading figure in the study of obesity, has proposed that they rely to an unusual extent on external, non-physiological factors in their eating behaviour. In one of his experiments, obese and normal subjects sat in a room in which the clock had been set either fast or slow. They were offered lunch, having been deceived into thinking that they were eating either earlier or later than usual. The obese individuals were found to be far more influenced by the clock than the others, and they actually ate *less* than their slimmer colleagues when they thought they were eating earlier than usual.

Fat people may be more influenced by external factors (the taste of food, for example) but they are less able to recognise stomach contractions and other internal signs of hunger. Unlike other people, they do not eat less when they are afraid or anxious. Other findings are that obese Jews find the Yom Kippur fast less taxing than those with normal eating habits so long as they remain in the synagogue and away from the sight of food, and that obese aircrews suffer relatively little disruption of their eating patterns as a result of jet-lag.

At mealtimes, obese people eat distinctively: they take larger mouthfuls, have shorter intervals between one mouthful and the next, and interrupt their eating to talk or put their fork down less frequently. A recent observational study of American children aged between four and twelve confirmed that this pattern is established in childhood – fat children eat more, quicker, and chew their food less. This study raises an interesting dilemma for parents, because it may be that telling children not to play with their food and to eat up quickly encourages later obesity. However, although we know that obesity is accompanied by fast eating, it is not established that fast eating leads to obesity. Nor is it only fat people who eat fast, as you can see from observing the eating habits of anyone who has spent any time in a boarding-school or other institution where second helpings go to those who finish first.

By definition, obesity is damaging to health. What are the

chances of curing it? Research shows that 97 per cent of those who go on a diet will return to their old weight or even have added a few pounds within a year. Of course many slimmers are not actually obese, but the picture is not an encouraging one. There are many treatments available to the obese. Behavioural methods, in which you first have to record the circumstances in which you eat, and then learn to limit your exposure to stimuli associated with food and to reward yourself for meeting certain targets of weight reduction, are probably the most effective, especially when you are also taught how to change your eating habits.

Other methods are less successful. Individual psychotherapy, hypnosis and supportive group methods are all used in the treatment of obesity, to little effect. Dieting leads to a short-term loss of weight, but this is rarely sustained unless it is part of a programme of behavioural training. In extreme cases, food starvation is sometimes used in a carefully controlled hospital setting, but the risk here is that it will lead to new psychological problems. More traditional medical methods are also of doubtful value. The long-term prognosis when appetite-reducing drugs such as amphetamines ('speed') are used is poor, and there is a risk of becoming dependent on them or of undergoing a change of personality. Such drugs may be a useful crutch to help change eating habits, but their use on a long-term basis may lead to more harm than good. A more drastic solution is surgery which causes the small intestine to be partially bypassed, thereby reducing its absorptive capacity. This leads to a dramatic loss of weight, but the operation is dangerous – occasionally even fatal – and it has unpleasant side-effects like diarrhoea, flatulence and loss of hair; it should only be performed in cases of intractable massive obesity.

Generally, all these treatments are depressingly unsuccessful. No more than 25 per cent of obese people who enter treatment lose as much as twenty pounds, and only 5 per cent lose as much as forty pounds. The most effective approach involves behavioural management and environmental control, because this places the emphasis on teaching patients how to change their eating habits permanently. But our best hope of reducing the incidence of obesity must lie in the development of appropriate eating habits in children and – especially – in ensuring that they are not overfed during the vital first year of life.

Reluctant eaters

At the other extreme of eating disorders is the much rarer condition called *anorexia nervosa*, the compulsion to lose weight that can lead to serious or even fatal self-starvation. Obese people may envy individuals who have anorexia, and there is a link between the two diseases: many anorectics have previously been obese. Generally speaking, anorexia is a condition which afflicts young middle-class women. The average age of onset is about seventeen, and it is more common in Britain amongst girls at independent boarding-schools than at state schools. Recently, however, a case was reported of a woman showing the classic symptoms – a preoccupation with the shape of the body and an irrationally strong urge to slim by dieting, purging and vomiting – for the first time at the age of fifty-two, and the disease is not unknown in men. The causes of anorexia remain obscure. It may be a reaction to the affluence and over-eating in our society. It may also reflect pressures from the media on teenage girls to follow slimming diets, and the prevalence of psychological problems associated with adolescent self-consciousness. Once again, the most effective treatment involves behavioural training, perhaps in combination with controlled feeding and some psychotherapy in hospital. But since eating too much or too little are both habits which are extremely difficult to break, it is clear that the best way of avoiding eating problems is to prevent them developing in the first place.

4 Sleeping

The innocent sleep,
Sleep that knits up the ravell'd sleave of care,
The death of each day's life, sore labour's bath,
Balm of hurt minds, great nature's second course,
Chief nourisher in life's feast.

Macbeth's musings introduce a number of popular views about the nature of sleep. When we say that someone is sleeping like a baby, we are referring not only to the fact that babies spend the majority of their lives asleep, but also to the belief that whatever mischief we may get up to while awake, we can do – and come to – little harm so long as we are sleeping. We believe strongly in the restorative value of sleep. After a hard day's work, whether physical or intellectual, we go to bed worn out and wake up feeling refreshed. If we suspect that we are about to become ill we go to bed early. And because a shortage of sleep or disruption of our normal sleeping habits makes us feel jaded, we are ready to accept that sleeping is a biological necessity. We would also probably be happy to follow Shakespeare in treating night-time as a punctuation mark between the days in which the action of our life takes place, and would certainly not dispute the idea that while asleep we somehow gain sustenance to see us through the next day. This way of thinking about sleep has not been shown to be wrong. It is, however, very difficult to see how it can be right. But before considering why we need sleep and examining what happens when we are forced to go without it, we must first understand what takes place during the course of a night's sleep.

What is sleep?
Sleep can be defined as a recurrent, healthy state of inertia

during which our ability to react to what is going on around us is greatly reduced. It is therefore different from a hypnotic trance, in which responsiveness to the external stimulus of the hypnotist's voice is not diminished, and it can be distinguished, by various physiological measures, from the altered state of consciousness which is induced by meditation. One such measure is the *electroencephalogram* (EEG), which has become the sleep researcher's main tool. The passage of nerve impulses and other electrochemical events in nerve cells are accompanied by tiny changes in electrical potential, and these can be recorded from electrodes which are placed on the surface of the head without causing any discomfort to the sleeper. The electrical events are of very low voltage, so are fed into an amplifier until they become sufficiently powerful to move a pen on a copying-machine known as a *polygraph* (the 'lie detector' is a polygraph wired up to measure small changes in electrical activity on the surface of the skin which indicate nervousness); in this way the brain's activity can be recorded.

There are four major brain rhythms in human adults, each associated with different frequencies of electrical activity. Beta rhythm, which is seen when we are awake and active, refers to activity of 14–25 cycles per second. Alpha rhythm is slower, between 8 and 13 cycles per second, and occurs when we are awake but relaxing with our eyes closed. As we lie in bed and become drowsy, activity in the alpha band gives way to theta rhythm, in which irregular low-voltage waves of 4–6 cycles per second are accompanied by rolling movements of the eyeball. This is the first stage of sleep. In the second stage, higher-voltage waves in the same frequency band are broken by bursts of much higher frequency activity (12–14 cycles per second). In stages three and four, deep or *slow-wave sleep* (SWS), there is a predominance of high-voltage activity of low frequency (one or two cycles per second). Together, these four stages are known as *orthodox sleep*, and they account for about three-quarters of the time we spend asleep as adults. During them, breathing, heart-rate and blood pressure are regular, the flow of blood in the brain is reduced, and brain temperature falls slightly.

Orthodox sleep is also sometimes called *non-rapid eye movement sleep* (NREM) to distinguish it from the activity in which we spend the remaining 25 per cent of our time asleep. *Rapid eye movement sleep* (REM) is characterised by low-voltage EEG in the 4–10 cycles per second band, accompanied by bursts of rapid movements of the eyes. It is also called *paradoxical sleep*, because it reverses the trend of the preceding four stages of orthodox sleep in which the EEG becomes increasingly slower but more powerful as we fall into ever-deeper sleep. In REM sleep, breathing, heart-rate and blood pressure are irregular, and there are many more jerky movements of the face and body. Most muscles become flaccid, though the penis often becomes erect. The legs no longer respond to electrical stimulation (in orthodox sleep, the normal reflexes are present), the flow of blood through the brain is even greater than when we are fully awake, and brain temperature rises. It is popularly held that REM sleep is the time when we dream.

The diagram on p. 47 shows how a young adult passes through the various stages of sleep during a typical night. At other times in life the pattern is rather different. Babies sleep for about fourteen hours out of every twenty-four, and may spend half that time in REM sleep, or as much as three-quarters if they are born prematurely. In old age, both the total time spent asleep and the proportion of REM sleep is reduced. You can see from the graph that throughout the night we move from one stage to the next in a cyclical fashion. Four periods of REM sleep can be seen to occur at intervals of about one and a half hours, and the majority of REM sleep occurs in the second half of the night. The opposite is true for the slow-wave sleep of stages 3 and 4. There are only two or three periods of SWS, and they are usually confined to the first half of the night's sleep. In lower animals it is not always possible to divide sleep into these five neat stages, but REM sleep has been found in most species studied, and this has led researchers to assume that it is the fundamental, biologically necessary stage of sleep. In trying to establish why it is that we sleep, they have tended to focus their attention on REM sleep, ignoring the other stages. As we shall see, this may have been a mistake.

Why do we sleep?
Because some people need much less sleep than others (and a

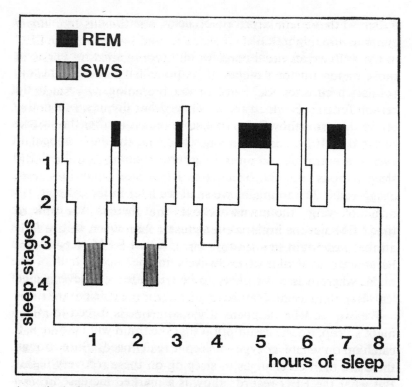

A typical night's sleep for a healthy young adult. Notice the cyclical movement from one stage to the next. A majority of rapid eye movement (REM) sleep is found in the second half of the night, while slow-wave sleep (SWS) occurs only in the first half of the night.

very few seem to need almost none), you might reasonably ask whether we actually *need* sleep at all. Perhaps it is a habit dictated by social convention rather than biological necessity? There are several reasons for doubting this. In the first place, sleep is a practice that we share with most other animals. True, some creatures like sharks and porpoises don't appear to sleep at all, and there is certainly great variety in sleeping habits between different species, related to other features of their life-style (whether they are predators or preyed-upon, for example). But the fact that most animals sleep is all the more striking because a sleeping animal is vulnerable to its enemies: since sleep has been retained through a long period of evolution it seems likely that it has some beneficial effects to compensate for the threat it presents for the survival of the species. Finally, we suffer when we are deprived of sleep, though not perhaps as much as you might think.

Do we have an equal need for all types of sleep, or are some more important than others? It is popularly believed that our primary need is for REM sleep, though opinions differ as to the reason for this. Some say that we need our dreams, others that REM sleep somehow helps to restore the brain after the stresses of the day. It has also been suggested that the day's important events are transferred into long-term memory during REM sleep periods. But the benefits of REM sleep may have been exaggerated. Dreaming, as we shall see later in the chapter, is a mixed blessing – though we all do it – and there is little evidence that REM sleep is involved in memory. Moreover, if it really is all that important, it's surely very odd that REM sleep should be concentrated almost exclusively in the *second* half of the night, where it is most likely to be truncated whenever we get less sleep than usual. Nature tends to be more efficient than this.

We can see what happens when someone is forced to miss a night's sleep, on the assumption that the brain will take steps to catch up on whatever type of sleep it really needs. Sure enough, there are marked changes in sleeping on these recovery nights. But what the EEG records show is a marked increase in *slow-wave sleep* rather than REM sleep in the first instance. There *is* what we might call a REM sleep rebound, but it only occurs after the SWS rebound has been satisfied. This was demonstrated in a recent experiment in which volunteer subjects were kept awake for more than eight days before finally being allowed to sleep. On the following three nights they increased the amount of time they spent in SWS by 350, 250 and 200 per cent respectively. During the same nights, time spent in REM sleep increased by 30, 60 and 20 per cent. So although we may have a need for REM sleep, it seems to be much less acute than our demand for SWS. As all these increases were achieved at the expense of stages 1 and 2, it looks as though the early stages of sleep are just a means of reaching the later stages.

In line with these findings, it is significant that people whose sleep is regularly limited spend a greater portion of their sleeping time in SWS, reducing not only the early stages but also REM sleep. Those of us who naturally seem to need little sleep show comparatively large amounts of SWS, but only small amounts of REM sleep. On the other hand, naturally *long* sleepers (those who spend significantly more than the average eight hours a day asleep) tend to spend the extra time in REM and stage 2 sleep, which suggests that REM sleep, far from being a biological necessity, may actually be a luxury. This view is confirmed by an experiment in which normal healthy sleepers were encouraged to take as much sleep as possible. On average, they managed an extra 1½–2 hours, made up almost entirely of REM and stage 2 sleep.

What is surprising about the effects of a *total* lack of sleep is that they are so small. After periods of up to a week without sleep, we may become slightly less efficient at simple tasks which require us to pay close attention, though even this is disputed. In most experiments on sleep deprivation, the volunteer subjects are kept awake and pleasantly entertained most of the time, and are only occasionally required to carry out tests to see if their efficiency has been impaired. So long as the task is sufficiently interesting, either because it is difficult or because a reward is offered for getting it right, the finding is that people perform very close to the level of efficiency they achieve with their normal quota of sleep. (This is just as well, since many workers in demanding and responsible jobs – doctors and pilots, for example – are regularly required to perform in conditions of partial if not total sleep deprivation.) In a less agreeable experiment, subjects were required to work continuously at a monotonous task for 48 hours, starting in the morning. In these conditions, performance fell off to 82 per cent of its original level in the small hours of the next morning. During the second day it picked up again to 96 per cent of the original level, only to fall again, this time by as much as a third, during the second night.

Lack of sleep leads to an increase in the production of the stress hormones adrenalin and nor-adrenalin. But this is difficult to interpret, because any physiological irregularities may just be a response to the novelty of going without sleep. Only if we define a stressor as anything which causes us to adapt to change – a very broad definition, though one which is quite widely accepted – can we say with confidence that going without sleep is stressful.

What is certain is that being kept awake for long periods has definite effects on our mood. To the extent that this affects our dealings with other people and hence our efficiency as social beings, it seems that being deprived of sleep influences our ability to deal with life. If we are deprived of REM sleep, we become increasingly irritable; if we are deprived of SWS, we become depressed and lethargic.

Talk of lethargy brings us close to popular ideas about sleep. If we miss a night's sleep, we can carry on at work the next day, but we may feel tired. In deciding when to go to bed, we are influenced both by how much we have done during the day (especially the amount of physical exercise we have taken), and by how long it is since we were last asleep. We have science on our side in only one of these beliefs. Within limits, the longer we have been awake the more SWS we take when we go to sleep. And if we take a nap in the afternoon, this significantly reduces the amount of SWS – but not REM sleep – which we take the following night, even if the nap contained more REM sleep than SWS.

Incidentally, the habit of taking an afternoon nap has much to commend it. We saw in the last chapter that there is a post-lunch dip in efficiency which affects us all. A recent experiment showed that students who were in the habit of napping not only speeded up their reactions but also improved their mood, when these were measured at five o'clock. The effects were equally marked whether the students had slept for two hours or only thirty minutes. We do not know whether the effects were maintained throughout the rest of the day, or whether this technique would work for people who are not habitual nappers, but we *do* know that the beneficial effects of a nap are much greater than those of just resting on a bed without going to sleep.

So far as the connection between exercise and sleep is concerned, popular belief may well be wrong. During SWS, the human growth hormone is produced in large quantities, and since the growth hormone aids protein synthesis and tissue growth, it has been assumed that the function of SWS is to restore the body. But this idea is difficult to maintain in the light of carefully controlled experiments which show that taking moderate to heavy exercise actually has no effect on the pattern of sleep. There is no increase in SWS unless the exercise is taken late in the day, and then it is more likely that the normal process of recovering from exercise is intruding into sleep than that we are showing increased need for SWS.

So what is the point of sleep, and of SWS in particular? There are a number of alternatives to the bodily recuperation theory. For example, the object of sleep may not be to restore energy but to conserve it. Perhaps sleep just keeps us inactive and ensures that we maintain a regular cycle of rest and activity, rather than offering any unique physiological benefits. Yet it is hard to shake off the feeling that sleep does us some direct good, and although Macbeth may have been mistaken in regarding it as sore labour's bath, the possibility remains that it is the balm of hurt minds.

A large proportion of the information with which the brain is bombarded during the day arrives by courtesy of the eye – about a third of all the nerve fibres entering the brain come from the eyes. One consequence of being deprived of sleep is that we become prone to visual disturbances: misperceptions and mild visual hallucinations are commonly reported after a few days without sleep. So although sleeping may have no generally restorative effect on our bodily processes, perhaps it serves a useful function by giving the visual system a chance to recover. But this can only be a partial explanation of why we sleep, because in the normal course of events people spend as much time in REM sleep as in SWS. REM sleep may be less vital, even a luxury, but we clearly cannot ignore it.

REM sleep and dreaming
In fact I wish we *could* ignore REM sleep, because it is an enigma. There is no shortage of theories about its function: the trouble is, none of them stand up. At the time of writing, in spite of an enormous research effort, we just don't know what the point of REM sleep is. I described it earlier as a time of intense internal activity, marked by an increase of blood flow in the brain, and pointed out that babies spend twice as high a proportion of their sleeping time in REM sleep as do adults. But these facts are open to many interpretations. For example,

it has been suggested that REM sleep is a time for increased protein synthesis, when repairs are made either to the body or the brain. But this proposal is difficult to reconcile with the pattern of recovery from sleep deprivation we have noted. Other researchers have suggested that REM sleep is a time for getting rid of surplus energy or *drive*, when undesirable substances (the mysterious 'dream hormones') are discharged into the blood, causing us to start dreaming. But this would hardly compensate for the fact that REM sleep is physically stressful; dreams not only reflect stress and anxiety but may well add to them, as anyone who has woken from a nightmare sweating with fear will know.

The most convincing account of the *evolutionary* significance of REM sleep suggests that its intense activity is a preparation for waking up, so that if we find ourselves threatened by an enemy who has crept up while we were in deep sleep, we will wake up in top gear, ready to run away or fight for our lives. On this analysis, the terrifying monsters of our dreams are interpreted as hallucinated versions of our enemies, and the function of dreaming is to save vital seconds adjusting to the situation when we wake up. It is an attractive theory, and one that can explain the occurrence of REM sleep in the second half of the night. But there are two fatal flaws. Not only do extremely vulnerable animals like rabbits actually spend a much smaller proportion of their sleeping time in REM sleep than predators such as cats and men, but – even more damaging to the theory – most animals share our practice, shown in the diagram on p. 47, of waking up from *non*-rapid eye movement sleep rather than from REM sleep. If REM sleep revs us up, it does so at the wrong time.

My earlier statement that we dream during REM sleep might have been misleading. It is true that when people are woken from REM sleep there is a very high probability that they will say they were dreaming, but they also sometimes report a dream when woken from non-REM sleep. However, REM-sleep dreams are more likely to be remembered than those of non-REM sleep, and eye movements may well reflect the events of a dream, since they occur more rapidly during a dream in which the dreamer plays an active part than one in which he is a passive observer. It has been suggested, not suprisingly, that the erections which almost always accompany REM sleep in men reflect the erotic content of their dreams, though there is another, less torrid, explanation. In infancy, an erection is a sign of generalised tension, provoked for example by taking the bottle away from the baby's mouth. The behaviour of the adult male in REM sleep may merely represent regression to earlier habits. It is also significant that sleep-walking and talking while asleep, both activities which are thought to indicate that the sleeper is dreaming, occur only in non-REM sleep.

We may engage in some form of mental activity all the time we are asleep, but it is very difficult to test the truth of this suggestion, because of the problem that bedevils all research into dreaming: for our basic data, we have to rely on people's memories of their dreams. These are certainly subjective, probably incomplete, and possibly distorted both in the recollection and the telling. In short, they would be unacceptable as scientific data were it not for the fact that they are all we have to work with.

We all know that people's ability to remember their dreams differs greatly – some people deny that they ever dream – and it has been suggested that this is related to other aspects of an individual's personality. The ability to recall dreams has been linked with an imaginative and flexible personality, while non-recallers (usually defined as those who remember less than one dream a month) are labelled as more rational but less imaginative. Research suggests that this identification is mistaken. It seems that we all dream, but that 'good' dream recallers are just those with the best visual memories in waking life, regardless of their personality. This is an interesting finding because not only does it confirm that dreams are visual phenomena (except for people who have been blind from birth, whose dreams involve only hearing, touch and smell), it also shows that waking and sleeping are not independent states.

The contents of our dreams are strongly influenced by our waking life: waking preoccupations and anxieties regularly intrude into dreams, often in such a direct and realistic fashion that there is no need for interpretation. The night after finishing the research for this section of the book, I – normally an unspectacular dreamer with poor recall – had a sequence of five vivid dreams, which exemplified one after the other the five most common types of dream, as described in the book I had just read. An impressive if somewhat ostentatious *tour de force* by my subconscious, and one which clearly reflected the anxiety with which I approached the task of writing about a confused and confusing topic.

So far as the interpretation of obscure dreams is concerned, if our waking and sleeping states are intimately connected it seems safe to accept much of our dreaming at face value. If you dream of making love with your neighbour's wife, the chances are that you fancy her. Similarly, many nightmares reflect waking fears and may include recognisable unpleasant memories. But science at present has nothing to offer when it comes to the pursuit of symbols or the unravelling of metaphors in dreams. Dream interpretation has been flourishing for at least 7000 years without producing any generally accepted method for the translation of dream material, nor is there any sign of such a thing in the near future. Any dream may be interpreted in quite different ways by two 'expert' interpreters, each following the precepts of his particular school, and I know of no empirical evidence which supports one approach at the expense of any other.

We know that dreaming is associated with anxiety, but it is still uncertain whether dreams reduce or add to the level of our anxiety. The controversy reflects the two very different sources of man's interest in dreams, an interest which dates back at least to 5000 B.C. – we still have dream books compiled at that date. Originally, dreams were examined for their religious significance: the Egyptians regarded them as messages from the gods, the Chinese as communications from the soul. But in addition to this mystical approach there is also a long tradition of using dreams for medical diagnosis. This can be traced back at least as far as Hippocrates, the father of medical science, who believed that dreams were directly related to a patient's physical condition: dreams of barren trees, for example, he took to indicate an insufficiency of sperm. Both traditions are still alive, and their contemporary exponents have opposite views not only about the connection between dreaming and anxiety but also about the more fundamental question, is dreaming good for us?

The mystical approach to dreaming represents it as a beneficial process. Dreams are described as the thoughts of the heart, which tend to be ignored under the pressures of our waking lives but which can reveal hidden talents, offer insights into what preoccupies us consciously and unconsciously, and help us to face challenges. The suggestion is that dreams enable us to come to grips with problems which would be intolerable in the harsh spotlight of conscious experience had they not previously been explored in the more muted light of the subconscious. At the other extreme, doctors can point to the stressful nature of REM sleep – they liken it to a storm – and the fact that nightmares produce all the physiological indices of anxiety. Stress is known to exacerbate both physical and mental illness, which suggests that dreaming is far from beneficial. It has even been proposed that people who die in their sleep are killed by their dreams.

This is the sort of argument which ought to be resolvable by experiments. We know that the contents of dreams can be influenced both by suggestions made to the sleeper before he drops off and by words spoken into his ear during REM sleep. These facts were exploited in a recent experiment which seems to provide a convincing test of the notion that dreaming helps us to adapt to stress. Subjects were shown a chillingly effective propaganda film about industrial accidents, which included close-up shots of a finger being sawn off and of a workman dying in great pain, impaled by a piece of timber. They saw the film before going to sleep in the laboratory and again first thing the next morning, and on both occasions were asked to say how stressful they found it. During the night the film's sound-track was played to half of the subjects while they were in REM sleep, and all subjects were required to write detailed reports of their dreams. As expected, those who heard the sound-track while they were asleep incorporated more of the film's events into their dreams. But – contrary to expectation – these subjects found the second viewing of the film *more* distressing than those who had not dreamt about it. This experiment clearly offers no support for the idea that dreaming helps us to cope with stress. Instead, we are left with the darker view that dreams may be a cause rather than just a consequence of anxiety – murderous slumber rather than sweet repose.

As a footnote to this conclusion, it is interesting to note that sleep deprivation has been successfully used to treat people with severe depression. Psychotic depression sometimes lifts towards the end of the day, only to fall again during sleep. Keeping patients awake throughout the night allows the good mood of the evening to be sustained, and this has been found an effective form of treatment for some severely depressed patients who have failed to respond to other forms of therapy. It may also be significant that people who since childhood have regularly taken more than nine hours sleep a night not only spend a large portion of the extra sleeping time in REM sleep, but are also unusually prone to anxiety and depression. This might be explained by saying that anxious people need more dreaming in order to help them cope with their anxieties. I suggest an equally plausible explanation is that naturally long sleepers are made more anxious as a result of the extra time they spend dreaming.

Practical considerations

Many social conventions surround sleeping, no less than eating. Sleeping is one of our most private habits, which may explain not only why bedrooms are furthest from the front door, but also why it is considered so rude to fall asleep at the dinner table. It is an abuse of the privilege of privacy which being asleep confers, quite apart from the fact that it allows us to display in public the anti-social aspects of sleeping – snoring, scratching, grunting and so on – which we normally inflict only on our most intimate companions. In this context we might speculate on the implications of the expression 'sleeping with': is it merely a euphemism, or does the act of copulation acquire extra significance when lovers share the further intimacy of sleeping in the same bed?

For many people, the difficulty of explaining sleep and dreams is trivial in comparison with the practical problem of getting to sleep. Insomnia is by far the most common sleeping disorder – there can be hardly an adult who has not suffered from it at some time – and it accompanies most forms of mental stress. This might seem to reinforce the argument that sleep provides relief from stress were it not for the fact, cited above, that deliberately depriving severely depressed people can make them better rather than worse. In fact, the ill effects of insomnia may be due less to lack of sleep as such than to the anxiety which people feel as they lie tossing and turning, unable to sleep. Will I be too tired for work tomorrow? Why can't I sleep when it's one in the morning and I am exhausted? These are the worries that send so many people to their doctors for sleeping pills. But doctors have become less willing to prescribe hypnotic drugs because of the dangers of addiction and side-effects. Modern sleeping pills like Mogadon are far less dangerous than old-fashioned barbiturates, but the best way to deal with insomnia is often simply to accept it.

Instead of lying in the dark fretting, you should get up and put the extra time you have gained to good use. If you are unable to get to sleep, it may be that you don't need to; different people require different amounts of sleep, and you should not take seriously the old joke that the amount of sleep required by the average person is about half an hour more. Unfortunately, such considerations do not reassure all insomniacs, especially those who do not enjoy reading and other quiet activities that can be pursued in the middle of the night. If you fall into this category, you may find it more fruitful to attack the problem by learning how to relax and hence to get to sleep. There are a number of different types of relaxation training which can greatly improve the lot of chronic insomniacs, so long as the training is carried out by a skilled therapist (just telling an insomniac to relax without teaching him how to do so is no use). Two of the most successful techniques are *progressive relaxation*, where you learn to reduce your level of physiological arousal by becoming more aware of the actions of your muscles, and *autogenic relaxation*, in which you engage in a sort of self-hypnosis, silently repeating over and over the suggestion that various parts of your body are warm and becoming heavy. By learning to relax, you can cure your own insomnia. We shall see later in the book that 'self-help' is a feature of most modern treatments of neurotic disorders, and relaxation training may be a more effective way of overcoming insomnia than sleeping pills.

5 Smiling

What's in a smile?

If you doubt that smiling is an important habit, try a couple of simple experiments. First, take a close look at your own face in a mirror, and then compare what you see with a photograph of yourself as an adolescent. Some of the changes will be idiosyncratic: you may have grown a moustache or acquired lasting scars from a car crash. But if you want a more accurate idea of what your face has been doing in the years since the picture was taken, concentrate on the new lines which have appeared, because these have been formed by use. You will find that the deepest are the laughter lines which curl away from the bottom of your nose and end somewhere beneath the lips. If this surprises you (you may think that you don't often smile) it is because smiling is rarely a deliberate, consciously directed action – which is in fact its greatest strength. Smiling is perhaps the most powerful single technique for non-verbal communication (NVC) we possess, precisely because the effectiveness of NVC, or 'body-language', lies in the fact that its signals are outside the full conscious awareness of the person who is sending them. The ambiguity and subtlety of NVC signals increases their impact, and may on occasions make them more useful than spoken language in telling other people what we feel about them.

If this seems implausible, try another experiment. Talk to someone without allowing yourself to smile; you will find this difficult, but possible. What will be less easy is getting the same person to talk to you again, because there is something decidedly unnerving about a conversation with someone who never smiles.

The great advantage of the ambiguity of NVC is that if the message it conveys doesn't please the person at whom you are directing it, you can always claim that they have misunderstood you. Suppose you laugh when someone is telling you about a misfortune he has suffered, and he reacts coldly, saying that it is no laughing matter. You can then protest that you weren't laughing *at* him (ridicule), but *with* him (sympathy). Unlike smiling, laughter is in fact rarely used to express sympathy, but you still have a much better chance of retrieving the situation than if you had committed to words your true sentiment: that you find it extremely funny that he has broken his leg ski-ing. Both smiling and laughter have this ambiguity, and it is no accident that smiling involves the laughter lines. So far as the movement of muscles is concerned the two activities are very similar, laughing being a more intense form of smiling. But when we study the circumstances in which people smile or laugh, it becomes clear that the two are not completely interchangeable.

What is the meaning of a smile? When a human adult smiles, he may be indicating any one or more of at least six different things. The following description of an imaginary social worker's morning illustrates some of them. Before seeing his first client, we find him sitting in his office, looking at the pleasant view from his window, and smiling. He saw a good film last night, slept well, and is thinking how much happier he is in his job than his brother-in-law. His smile is a simple expression of *happiness*. But when the first client of the morning arrives, his expression becomes noticeably exaggerated as he assumes the professional smile which is designed to convey both *sympathy* with the client's problem and *reassurance* that he is in good hands. Details of the saga which is then related are clearly meant to be funny, so the social worker smiles to show mild *amusement*. But the story also contains some elements which are frankly improbable, and a sardonic smile betrays incredulity and even *ridicule* (Aw, come *on*!). The advice given by our social worker turns out to be inappropriate, so later we find him explaining to his boss what went wrong. Now his smile is sheepish, a gesture of appeasement and *submission*.

These types of smile are distinct, but they all serve to oil the wheels of everyday social intercourse. Smiling is particularly useful in conveying a recognition of status, often being a tacit acceptance of the smiler's inferiority. Since most social animals seem to establish hierarchies of dominance and relative status, it comes as no surprise to find that the physical characteristics of the human smile – lips retracted and teeth partially bared – closely resemble the expression adopted by chimpanzees when they want to indicate submission (they also smile as an overture of friendship). Observation of children in nursery schools confirms that their patterns of smiling are related to position in the pecking-order of the group: they smile more at children who are older than them. At this age, incidentally, children do not laugh at other people's misfortunes, as adults may – they simply watch them. Laughter in young children accompanies violent physical activity, and it may actually be more closely related to screaming than to smiling.

Smiling and laughter

For adults, laughter shares some but not all of the functions of smiling. We chortle with glee (which can mean either amusement or happiness) and laugh to express strong ridicule, but laughter is rarely used to demonstrate sympathy or submission (laughing at the boss's jokes may be an exception). Instead, we tend to use it as a competitive weapon to assert dominance – we laugh to gain attention or to demonstrate self-confidence – or alternatively to imply that we belong in a group. But perhaps the main function of laughter is to indicate that things are not to be taken seriously. Now this may sound trite, but it has important implications. It means that laughter allows considerable licence in what is being said: in theory, you should be able to say the most offensive things to people so long as you remember to accompany your observations with a laugh. In practice, the protective properties of laughter are limited, and I wouldn't recommend that you push this principle too far.

There are other ways in which we can use laughter as a signal. For example at the beginning of a party where few people know each other, the guests may gather into silent and embarrassed groups. If the host feels obliged to come over and break the ice, he is quite likely to announce his arrival on the outskirts of a group with a determined laugh. Taken at face value, this is an extraordinary piece of behaviour. Nothing in the circumstances seems to justify it: there is nothing to laugh at. We might be less surprised if he wept. But we don't assume that he is mad, or totally devoid of social skills. On the contrary, his manoeuvre is often successful, because laughter is such a powerful signal that it can create artificially an atmosphere in which its spontaneous expression no longer seems at all out of place.

In view of the importance of non-verbal communication in our dealings with other people, it is not surprising that smiling is a habit which has attracted the attention of social psychologists. It is well known that patterns of behaviour are influenced by the social class of the participants, and smiling is no exception. In an experiment carried out at a large railway station in London, an actor playing the role either of a middle-class or a working-class commuter sought directions from passers-by. Dressed in a business suit and equipped with hat and umbrella, he elicited smiles from members of his own apparent class (especially as they finished replying to his query), but not from members of the working class. When cast in a working-class role, he was smiled at by members of neither class.

What happens when the expression on your face contradicts the content of what you are actually saying? Can you for example soften the blow of bad news by delivering it with a reassuring smile? In a recent American experiment, student volunteers were asked to watch videotape films of people conveying either pleasant or disturbing information, with either appropriate or inappropriate facial expressions. It was found that when they had been exposed to a conflict between the words and the facial expression, viewers made no attempt to resolve it by finding an explanation for the discrepancy. Instead, they were always more influenced by whichever was more disturbing, the words of the message or the speaker's expression. The experimental setting was rather artificial, but this finding certainly suggests that if you have an unpleasant message to deliver there is not much point in trying to sugar the pill by assuming a reassuring smile: it will be ignored.

I began this chapter by saying that smiling gains greatly from the fact that it is rarely a deliberate activity. But it can be so, and often the intention of the smiler is to deceive. In order to thwart him, you must be able to recognise a false smile. Experiments suggest that the best way to do this is to watch the area around the smiler's eyes: if it remains unwrinkled and the eyelids fail to narrow, beware. Other warning signals are an exaggerated raising of the upper lip to retract the corners of the mouth, and – sometimes – squaring of the lower lip without the jaw being moved forward. (If, in the absence of any of these warning signs, you are still doubtful of the smile's sincerity, perhaps you should make sure that the object of your suspicion hasn't read this chapter before you.)

Smiling and learning

In adults, then, smiling is an extremely versatile technique of non-verbal communication, and without it we would be greatly handicapped in our dealings with other people. But smiling isn't just a device for ingratiating yourself with the boss or helping a conversation along: it once played a vital part in turning you into a person worth employing or talking to in the first place. A baby's smile often means something very different from the smile of an adult (though in certain circumstances adults may regress to the childhood pattern): in early life, smiling is not just a useful social skill but an essential prop for normal development.

The earliest smile usually appears soon after birth, and it occurs *endogenously*, that is without any stimulation from the outside world. It consists merely of a turning up of the corners of the mouth, has nothing to do with feeding, and probably arises as a result of spontaneous discharge from the central nervous system. It occurs almost exclusively in rapid eye movement (REM) sleep, and never when the baby has recently been startled. In the last chapter we saw that new-born babies spend much of their time in REM sleep, and that during REM sleep in adulthood there is possibly a discharge of surplus energy from the central nervous system. The emergence of smiling seems to dovetail neatly with those findings.

Later in the first week of life, you may *elicit* the same faint smile from the sleeping baby, by light touches on sensitive areas or by blowing on his skin; a week later, you can for the first time coax a slightly broader smile from him when he is awake, though glassy-eyed and drowsy (intoxicated) after feeding. At this stage, a high-pitched human voice is the most effective agent for producing a smile, though there may be a delay of about seven seconds before the baby smiles. It is not until the third week that the first *alert* smile appears, usually in response to the voice of the baby's mother, and his mouth is now pulled into a recognisable grin which is accompanied by a brightening and crinkling of the eyes. By week four, the baby is prepared to smile at a silent moving face or in response to the pat-a-cake routine, but it is not until he is about nine weeks old that a stationary face consistently produces a smile. This is a major developmental landmark, because for the first time the baby is showing that he can recognise something just by looking at it. Only at this point does it make sense to regard smiling as a social activity. Whatever mothers may think, there is no evidence that their babies can distinguish them from anyone else during the first weeks of life.

In these first weeks, babies smile when they become aroused beyond a certain point, whether as a result of spontaneous internal activity or in response to stimulation from the outside world. The most likely function of smiling at this stage is to release tension which has gradually built up. As the months go by and the baby learns to recognise more objects, he is most likely to smile at the sight of something unfamiliar or the occurrence of something unexpected: once an object has become familiar, he no longer smiles when it appears. Initially, tension is introduced by physical stimulation; later, when the baby has had a chance to develop expectations about the world, by the unexpected. But whatever its origins, the tension can be released by smiling.

In order to survive, we must be able to deal with uncertainty. To this end, one of our most powerful reflexes – the *orienting response* – comes into play whenever we encounter a novel or unexpected situation: our senses are directed towards the novel object, and a host of physiological changes (slower heart-rate, increased blood supply to the brain, reduction of muscle activity, the blocking of alpha rhythm in the brain, to name just a few) all combine to heighten our capacity to analyse what confronts us. The growing child *needs* regular exposure to novelty in order to develop intellectually, and this is why smiling is essential. By smiling when he is confronted with something new, the child can continue to inspect it, at the same time showing that he is no longer afraid but pleased and so encouraging the person looking after him to continue or repeat whatever it is that has engaged his attention (the orienting response is also known as the attentional response). The growing child also needs to meet new people if he is to be able to handle the intensely social world of childhood and adulthood, and during the second half of his first year of life he will begin to smile at strangers.

As smiling in babies seems to follow a *gradual* rise in tension, so laughter occurs in response to a *sudden* increase in tension, in infancy as in later life. A child first laughs at about four months old, when he receives vigorous physical stimulation – tickling, for example – or hears an unfrightening loud voice ('I'm going to GET you!'). Over the next two months it takes progressively less vigorous physical stimulation to make him laugh, and he also begins to respond to more subtle provocation (peek-a-boo, for example). This trend continues over the rest of the first year, with incongruity becoming an increasingly important source of merriment: the sight of his mother imitating the walk of a penguin or sticking her tongue out at him can now produce paroxysms of mirth, whereas earlier they would have been more likely to lead to tears.

By the age of seven or eight, children are amused not only by things that look funny, but also by things that sound odd. As they come to understand logic, they are delighted by stories containing logical incongruities or howlers. Take the following story:

Johnny's mother walked into a restaurant and ordered a whole cake to eat. When the waitress asked whether she wanted the cake cut into four or eight pieces, she replied: 'Just cut it into four. I'm trying to lose weight.'

This story infringes the principle of invariance, which says that things can remain the same in some essential respect – volume or weight, for example – even though they may be made to look different. When the story is told to children of different ages, those who find it funniest are those who have recently mastered the principle of invariance.

Both smiling and laughter are associated with the release of tension in children, and smiling at least seems to play a vital role in intellectual and social development. Smiling in adulthood is also related to tension and unpredictability. When our imaginary social worker in the previous section smiled at his boss as he admitted a mistake, I described his smile as sheepish and submissive. But it was also of course a nervous smile, reflecting the anxiety and tension which had built up while he awaited – uncertainly – his boss's reaction. Similarly, the laughter of a horror-film audience may be directly related to the amount of tension created, though hardened horror-movie buffs might deny it.

The importance of unpredictability in raising a laugh becomes clear when we consider the old conundrum, why can't we tickle ourselves? Student teachers in London recently took part, no doubt with due solemnity, in a carefully controlled laboratory experiment designed to establish the conditions in which tickling is most effective. They were tickled in a variety of different ways, and rated each experience for ticklishness on a seven-point scale, which varied from 'extremely' to 'not at all'. It was shown that, to achieve maximum impact, tickling should be carried out by another person at irregular intervals, with the victim having his eyes closed. Being able to see the feather coming or administering it oneself removes the element of unpredictability, and both are found to detract significantly from the experience of being tickled.

Smile and the world smiles with you
If smiling is not merely a useful social accomplishment but actually an essential habit, you might expect it to be universal, in the sense of being used and interpreted in roughly the same way all over the world. Californian psychologist Paul Ekman spent ten years testing this assumption. He visited thirteen different literate countries throughout the world and two remote, preliterate tribes in New Guinea, showing people photographs of actors with various facial expressions and asking them what they thought the person in the picture was feeling. In all the cultures surveyed, more than nine out of ten adults and children were able to interpret correctly a happy smile.

Not only do we almost always recognise the significance of the smiling face of a stranger, we are also likely to be influenced to a surprising extent by the expression on our own face, if this has been artificially manipulated. In another American experiment, student volunteers were informed – falsely – that they were taking part in an investigation of the movement of facial muscles during perception. After phoney electrodes had been attached to their face, they were given instructions to contract their muscles in such a way that they eventually were wearing either a smile or a frown. They then had to look at a picture, and were asked to fill in a checklist of adjectives to describe how they felt. A number of subjects guessed the real purpose of the experiment, but of the remainder, the smilers reported that they felt elated, even when the picture they saw had unpleasant connotations (the Ku-Klux-Klan in action), while the involuntary frowners felt angry even after viewing a picture of children playing inoffensively. So smiling can not only be used to convey what you are feeling, it can actually influence how you feel, and even give rise to feelings which are inappropriate to the real situation.

Fortunately for businessmen and diplomats smiling seems to be a universal language, although cross-cultural investigations have revealed some traps. The Japanese, for example, try to maintain an expressionless poker-face at all times. They consider the overt display of anger or grief a solecism, and sometimes use smiling or even laughter to disguise these emotions. The quick flash of the eyebrows which we add to a smile when we want to greet a friend at a distance, especially when we are talking to someone else, is also open to serious misinterpretation. In Anglo-Saxon cultures this gesture is occasionally used as a mild flirtation; in Japan, it is always regarded as indecent. In an attempt to avoid misunderstandings, social psychologists in America and Britain have begun to devise training programmes to instruct export salesmen and others in the ways of those with whom they are to deal, and these Culture Assimilator programmes have already proved their worth. Cross-cultural differences may seem to weaken the claim made by ethologists that smiling is an innate skill. But since it occurs in babies born not only blind but also without arms (and hence without the ability to learn facial expressions either by watching or touching other people's faces), it looks as though smiling, although it may be distorted by cultural filters, is an innate, universal piece of behaviour.

6 Liking

200 million Americans want to leave some things a mystery, and right at the top of those things we don't want to know is why a man falls in love with a woman and vice versa   U.S. Senator William Proxmire, 1975, commenting on a National Science Foundation grant for research into love

With respect, Senator, I doubt it. Unless magazine editors have got it badly wrong, there are few things in which we are more interested than the reasons why we like or love some people and dislike others. Physical attraction has obvious survival value for the species, but although the desire to have children may often be an important factor in a couple's decision to live together or to get married, I doubt whether it will get us far in trying to explain why we like each other. In this chapter I shall be looking at two fundamental questions: why do we make friends, and whom do we make friends with? You may share Senator Proxmire's view that this is not an area we need to study – surely we can all make friends and organise social relationships naturally, without any help from a psychologist? If you believe this, I suggest you have a word with a psychiatrist, marriage counsellor or anyone involved with industrial relations. I think they will confirm that making and keeping friends is not something we are naturally good at – indeed, the disruption of social relationships is one of the most frequent causes of psychological problems. Research indicates that friendship is a more complex business than you might expect.

Why do we make friends?
Although I don't believe that our liking people can be explained by an innate need either to produce children or to form a

permanent pair-bond as Desmond Morris suggests in *The Naked Ape*, I certainly don't want to rule out biological factors or to deny that liking is a necessity. We probably have an affiliation drive, similar in some respects to the more familiar biological drives of hunger and thirst, and certainly suffer when we are deprived of friends. But I would suggest that the need which this drive reflects is for stimulation or arousal, rather than for children or for a monogamous relationship. It is part of a more general curiosity or exploratory drive, the value of which was described in the last chapter.

However, adaptive considerations and biological drives are only part of the story. Friends fulfil another very important function: they serve to support the image we have of ourselves, and to confirm the value and rightness of the attitudes we hold. We project ourselves and our opinions on to friends – a number of experiments show that we judge our friends to be more like us than they really are – and so use them to boost our own self-esteem. Our thinking seems to go something like this. Here is someone I like and respect; he is similar to me and shares my view of the world: I must be pretty good as well. We use friends as a sounding-board for new ideas, and may even model ourselves on them. Generally, we like our friends to be successful because their success boosts our status in the eyes of the world. But if the gap between their success and our own becomes so marked that people start saying 'You're not really a friend of X, are you?' then the friendship is likely to turn sour: reflected glory is one thing, jealousy quite another. When friends become too successful, it not only draws attention to our relative lack of success, but also destroys the essential similarity on which the friendship was based.

There is a problem here, because the two functions of friendship – as a source of stimulation on the one hand, and of reassurance on the other – appear to make opposite predictions about the sort of people we should choose as friends. If we want to be stimulated, we will presumably seek out people who are different from us so that we can be surprised by them, whereas if what we are after is support for our view of the world and reassurance that we are desirable, we need friends who are as similar as possible to ourselves. These two apparently conflicting attributes of the ideal friend are encapsulated in the proverbs about opposites attracting and birds of a feather flocking together. So the study of friendship not only has practical importance, it may also be able to show which of these contradictory pieces of folk-wisdom is actually closer to the truth.

Who are our friends?

Research on friendship has turned up a number of facts, often interesting and occasionally useful, but until recently little effort was made to produce a coherent explanation of liking. It was for example established that the average American college student has 5.6 friends (as opposed to the 4.2 accumulated by the average middle-aged Nebraskan), and that we have a higher regard for friends whom we previously disliked than for those about whom our feelings have remained constant (so much for devotion and loyalty, as the brother of the prodigal son discovered to his cost, some years earlier).

In the laboratory, an ingenious technique has been devised by the American psychologist Donn Byrne to investigate the similarity–complementarity argument. A subject is asked to fill in a questionnaire which gives the experimenter a good idea of his attitude towards life and his view of the world. He is then kept occupied while a phoney attitude chart is constructed. This chart is alleged to represent the attitudes of someone the subject has never met, but it is actually based on the subject's own replies to the questionnaire, and is fixed in such a way that the bogus stranger's attitudes resemble those of the subject to a lesser or greater extent. The subject is then shown the rigged scale, and asked for his opinion of the mythical stranger. The results are usually clear-cut. The more similar the bogus stranger's attitudes are to those of the subject, the more attractive he is judged; the more importance the subject attaches to the values about which he has been quizzed, the more potent is the appeal of similarity. This effect is a strong one: white Americans known to be racially prejudiced and in favour of racial segregation are found to be more attracted to imaginary black separatists than to white liberals.

But does this tell us anything about real life, where our

predilections for people we have never met are of limited interest (except to those who run computer dating agencies), and we select and retain friends on the basis of considerably more evidence than was made available to Dr Byrne's subjects? Computer dating, which brings together people on the basis of similarity of attitudes and personality, is in fact rather successful. The largest such agency in Europe claims that about three-quarters of their customers enjoy their first date sufficiently to arrange further meetings, and independent laboratory studies confirm that dates arranged on the basis of attitude similarity are more successful than those not so arranged, though the position is less clear where personality is concerned. Moreover, studies of the development of friendship generally confirm the finding of the laboratory studies: so far as attitudes are concerned, birds of a feather do stick together. In an investigation of the friendships which developed amongst first-year students living in a hostel, it was found that similarity of attitudes towards politics, religion, hobbies and aesthetics – measured by an attitude questionnaire when the students first arrived – was the most effective predictor of who would be friends with whom four months later. But the *initial* patterns of friendship had nothing to do with similarity of attitudes, and more detailed analysis shows that the matter is less simple than I have so far made it out to be.

If we look at friendships that have been established for different lengths of time, it becomes clear that we cannot yet bury the attraction of opposites. Several investigators have found that in friendships of less than six months' standing, dissimilarity rather than similarity of attitudes seems to be the rule, whereas long-standing friendships – those which have lasted more than a year – tend to be between people who share the same views. It therefore looks as though brief friendships are based on the attraction of opposites, while birds of a feather flock together on a more permanent basis. By having two different sorts of friend we can derive both stimulation and reassurance from friendship. We use a succession of 'new' friends to provoke and stimulate us with ideas which may be unfamiliar or unacceptable to us, and drop them when the tensions become too acute – much of their charm lies in the fact

70

that they are expendable. But we also have a small number of old faithfuls, who share our attitudes and can be relied upon to support and reassure us.

Why do some long-term relationships break up while others survive? The results of studies of pairings, both voluntary (married couples) and forced (student room-mates who have been arbitrarily thrown together), are in line with the rest of the evidence: similarity is a better omen than complementarity for a successful relationship, with one important qualification. In marriage, once the field has been narrowed down in such a way that couples tend to come from similar backgrounds and to share a broad range of attitudes and values, a certain amount of dissimilarity seems to be necessary for the relationship to survive. So although a broadly similar outlook on the world increases the likelihood that a relationship will survive, excessive similarity – experienced at close quarters and over a number of years – can breed contempt. It has also been found that when we *dis*like people, the intensity of our feeling increases the more like us they are. Desirable though similarity may be, it is clearly possible to have too much of a good thing.

On balance, however, the evidence suggests that we would be well-advised to select both friends and spouses who share our attitudes – in other words, people who *think* like us. But should we also be looking for people who *are* like us? Probably, although there is still some doubt about this. Studies which have tried to establish that the people we get on best with are those who resemble us in personality face the problem that an individual's personality is more difficult to measure than his attitudes (this may explain the results of the studies on dating mentioned earlier); there is also the question of what stage of a friendship we are concerned with. So far as initial feelings about new acquaintances are concerned, the finding is that we are attracted towards people who resemble us on such broad dimensions of personality as sociability, masculinity–femininity and tolerance. But established friends are often dissimilar on these rather gross measures of personality; instead, they are found to be alike in more subtle ways – the terms in which they judge things and their characteristic way of viewing the world, i.e. those aspects of personality which are most closely related to their attitudes. So the rule seems to be that we are initially attracted to people who at first glance seem to behave like us (at this stage we have nothing else to go on), but that the friendship will only survive if, when we get to know them better, they are found to share our view of the world, and can support the opinions we hold, especially about ourselves (our *self-concept*). This explanation of friendship is supported by an experiment in which students were asked not only to estimate their own and a friend's I.Q., but also to guess how their friend would estimate their own I.Q. The results were revealing: the students did not consider that they and their friends were particularly similar in intelligence, but they did expect their friends to share their estimate of their own I.Q., i.e. to support their self-concept; the more established the friendship, the more convinced they were that they received this support.

The fact that researchers have found it difficult to link friendship with similarity in personality may also reflect the complexity of an individual's personality: we have many facets, and so need a disparate group of friends to support them. This may explain why we often have two close friends who have little in common, and may indeed dislike each other; it can also account for the behaviour of people who consciously avoid bringing their different sets of friends together, and are upset to discover that friends belonging to different sets know each other.

The girl next door
So far I have suggested that you like people who share your attitudes and view the world in similar terms. These may be the most important determinants of a successful friendship, but they are not the only ones. Statistically, we are more likely to be friends with people who live near us and with those whom – for whatever reason – we meet most often, but I am not sure how much importance we should attach to these findings. One famous study of the patterns of friendship in a large block of flats seemed to show that people who lived nearest to the letter-box or the entrance to the lift had the most friends. But other researchers have found that although living close to people and meeting them frequently may mean that we get to know them

better, it does not guarantee that we shall like them: it is as likely to emphasise their undesirable qualities as their attractiveness. I suspect that the importance of propinquity may have been exaggerated by social scientists who believe in architectural determinism – the idea that our physical surroundings play a large part in shaping our lives. I also have a suspicion that the often-quoted statistic that more than half of the married couples in Seattle used to live within three miles of each other before they got married may tell us more about the mobility (or lack of it) of Seattlans than about the dynamics of liking and loving.

Exceptions to the rule
Physical attractiveness also influences our choice of friends. We prefer our friends of both sexes to be attractive and, where the opposite sex is concerned, physical appearance can blind us to the fact that people we like may resemble us in neither attitudes nor personality. But even here, similarity cannot be ignored: studies show that we tend to marry people who, in the eyes of dispassionate observers, are roughly our equivalent in attractiveness, and where there is a large discrepancy it is usually compensated for along some other dimension (wealth or social status, for example). This economic theory of marital choice may also apply to a lesser extent to our choice of friends, which can account for some of the more glaring exceptions to the principle that birds of a feather flock together.

It is not until mid-adolescence that we begin to use psychological concepts to judge other people, and so become able to form friendships based on genuine similarity. Earlier, judgements are based exclusively on physical attributes and friends are selected in a ruthlessly (and unrealistically) opportunist way, which explains why young children get through friends so rapidly. Girls start using psychological concepts before boys, but adolescence is a volatile period for both sexes, marked by dramatic changes in personality. Teenage romances tend to be short-lived because this month's soul mate has become an incomprehensible stranger by next month. Before puberty, we choose unsuitable friends; during adolescence, we need to change our friends in order to support us as we ourselves change.

73

By adulthood, however, friends have become an essential prop for our psychological well-being: it is no accident that the inability to make friends or the disruption of an important relationship is at the root of so many psychological problems. We are social animals, and we are blessed not only with self-awareness, but also with sufficient intelligence to appreciate that there are alternatives to our own view of ourselves and the world. Friends provide us with a reliable source of reassurance that neither we nor our opinions are seriously out of step.

7 Working

According to Thomas Carlyle, work is the grand cure of all the miseries and maladies that ever beset mankind (Voltaire made the more modest claim that it banished only the three great evils of boredom, vice and poverty). Others have spoken of the dignity of labour, but I suspect that most people if asked why they worked would reply that they did so out of economic necessity. In fact, there have been such dramatic historical changes in our attitude towards working that it is clearly not part of our genetic endowment. Both the Greeks and the Romans thought manual work a curse, suitable only for slaves, and the early Christians followed the Jewish tradition in considering it a punishment for man's original sin. But we are not Ancient Greeks or early Christians, so having accepted that attitudes towards work are socially and culturally determined, we need only consider the question of why we work in the context of the Protestant ethic, stemming from the teaching of Luther and Calvin, which is still predominant in modern Western industrial society. Actually, the harsher aspects of this doctrine, which are encapsulated in St Paul's edict, 'If any would not work, neither should he eat', have largely been abandoned; most countries now have welfare programmes which allow those who do not work – for whatever reason – to subsist.

The strange fact is that the last hundred years have seen not only the dehumanising of manual work, with the introduction of mass-production methods and 'scientific management', and a consequent reduction in the satisfaction which an individual can derive from the performance of a skilled craft, but also universal acceptance of the idea that everyone *ought* to work, even though they may have no absolute economic necessity to do so. Even those fortunate enough to inherit great wealth have been unable to resist the prevailing climate of opinion – it is not just a reduction in the number of people prepared to become Jeeveses which has led to the virtual extinction of Bertie Woosters – and a large proportion of those who suddenly find that they no longer have to work, after winning a lottery or the football pools, now choose to continue working, finding it too difficult to sustain a lifestyle which is not built around some form of work.

I don't think that we should be unduly impressed by surveys which claim to show that the vast majority of workers, even in what appear to be the most soul-destroying jobs, actually enjoy their work: the workers' response may just indicate that they are happy to be doing any job at all, rather than a positive feeling about their particular work. But we do seem to have reached a position where people prefer to work rather than not to work, and the reasons for this are complicated by the fact that different jobs seem to offer different sorts of rewards, while different people look for different types of satisfaction in their work. A basic tenet of the scientific management pioneered by Frederick Winslow Taylor at the end of the last century was that man the worker was a rational, economic creature, motivated only by his pay-packet. As the original Henry Ford put it, 'The average worker wants a job into which he does not have to put much physical effort. Above all, he wants a job in which he does not have to think'. What Ford thought the average worker *did* want can be deduced from the fact that he paid his workers a minimum wage which was more than twice the national average, and he would no doubt have regarded the reactions of a party of American automobile workers who recently visited the 'humanised' Saab-Scania engine plant in Sweden as proof that he needed no psychologists to tell him how to run his business. After watching their Swedish colleagues at work in a factory in which the traditional assembly line has been abandoned in favour of small groups of workers who are responsible for constructing a large section of the car rather than a single component, a device to increase job satisfaction, the Americans expressed a preference for the familiar Detroit assembly line, on the grounds that it allowed them to concentrate less, and to carry out their tasks in their sleep!

Money is certainly an effective motivator, but it is not the only reason why we work. There is no doubt that the economic motive can be overridden by other considerations: for example, even when they are being paid according to individual productivity, people tend to work at the same pace as those around them, and a number of studies have shown that the output of a team may actually fall when it gains a new member who refuses to accept the group norm and works at a faster rate. Being accepted as a member of a stable working group brings its own social reward, which may explain why many workers have mixed feelings about technological advances that remove them from the noise and dirt of the shop floor and leave them in splendid isolation, in charge of a machine which can carry out the tedious work they formerly did. It may also account for the behaviour of people who choose to work even though there is no economic necessity for them to do so – after all, it is not easy to be a playboy when there are so few people to play with!

But even more important than the economic and social factors which encourage us to work is the fact that many people find a sense of individual purpose in their work. People may say that they hate their work, but it matters to them, and their occupation makes an important contribution both to their image of themselves, and – particularly – to the way in which other people regard them. It is significant that when starting a conversation with strangers we begin by asking them what they do. Taken at its face value, this is a hopelessly general question: it would be quite legitimate for them to reply, 'I clean my teeth', or 'I put the milk bottles out every night'. But, in practice, they know exactly what we are after, and tell us that they are in plastics, or whatever. If they are out of work, they may reply that they don't do anything at the moment – doing has become a synonym for working – and it is a sad indication of the extent to which people's jobs have come to dominate our impression of them that this response may leave us very uncertain about how to continue the conversation. So not only does not working leave us short of cash and companionship, it also leads to social embarrassment, because of the hiatus left in the image we present to the world. Since the combination of economic and social factors may also severely damage the image we have of ourselves, it is hardly surprising to find that people prefer to

77

accept unpleasant or demeaning jobs rather than opt for the alternative of not working at all.

These considerations may help us to understand why we work at present, but it is essential to realise that our feelings about work are not immutable, for we shall certainly need to jettison our current attitude if the post-industrial society we have been promised (or threatened with) ever materialises. At the moment we seem to be in a confusing transitional period: behavioural scientists concerned with industrial problems are still trying to find ways of making us work harder, while at the back of their minds lurks the knowledge that they should also be preparing us for a time when there may be no work at all for many of us. The work ethos has become so firmly entrenched that it is difficult – and rather frightening – to contemplate a life without work, and the experience of firms whose advanced production methods have allowed them to test the water of the post-industrial era by offering their workers a significantly shorter working week, without any reduction in pay, is not altogether encouraging. However, the twin problems of adjusting to increased leisure and coping with the withdrawal pains of abandoning a habit which at present claims half our waking hours for most of our life, may become less formidable when everyone around us is in the same position. We can also take heart from the fact that our capacity to adapt to change has, in the past, seen us through no less revolutionary metamorphoses – for example, at the beginning of the industrial age. Given this capacity, and the fact that many of the individual characteristics which encourage us to work (the need for power and achievement, for example) seem to be culturally determined rather than inborn, I can see no insurmountable psychological barrier to stop us emulating the Greeks and the Romans by learning to adjust to life without work, should the circumstances ever demand it.

In short, although society, as it is at present constituted, offers us compelling reasons to work, I do not believe that we *must* work, in the sense that we must eat. On the other hand, there is very little evidence to support the view sometimes put forward that work is actually bad for us. Two very different types of work – shift work and the job of an executive – have caused alarm in medical circles over the last forty years or so, but in both cases the health risks seem to have been exaggerated. In the days when shift work was compulsory, it was associated with the incidence of gastric ulcers. But since it has become voluntary, this connection has disappeared, and there is no overall difference in health between shift-workers and others, as long as people who are not suited to shift work are allowed to opt out of it. Only a minority of the shift-workers at a Polish steelworks who took part in a recent survey said that they found working at night more fatiguing or disturbing than working the morning or afternoon shifts, and other researchers have found that shift work tends to increase the internal cohesion of working groups, which suggests that it may maximise the social rewards which work can offer. In line with this, absenteeism tends to be less of a problem among shift-workers than it is among day-workers.

So far as the much-publicised hazards of executive life are concerned, there is actually no evidence that long hours of work under high pressure are harmful, so long as the régime reflects a person's enthusiasm for what he is doing and leads to successful results. Thwarted ambition may lead to ulcers (though the evidence suggests that stress-linked illnesses may in fact be *less* prevalent in the boardroom than they are on the shop floor), but it is not only at work that one's ambitions are thwarted. The executive who smokes and drinks to excess, or disrupts the biological rhythms of his body by eating and sleeping irregularly, is certainly jeopardising his health, but work is not the culprit – he would be no less likely to end up in hospital if he spent the hours at the office or in aeroplanes reading novels, rather than working on company business. We know that prolonged exposure to any sort of adverse circumstances makes us more susceptible to anxiety, depression and a variety of chronic stress illnesses, and it can't be denied that many jobs contain elements which are stressful to certain types of individual. The sensible policy, therefore, is to recognise and accept the limitations of your own constitution and steer clear of working conditions you are ill-equipped to deal with. As I write this, a campaign has just begun to secure shorter working hours for British members of parliament, a proposal which has much to commend it, since at present they are required to make decisions at a time of the day when they are biologically least fit to do so. But it must be pointed out that politicians who dislike staying up all night are no less free than shift-workers to seek an occupation they find more congenial. In fact, the life expectancy of an MP compares favourably with that of people working in jobs with much shorter hours, which suggests that this self-selection procedure is already in effective operation.

Psychology and industry

Although psychologists have long been anxious to get to grips with a host of the theoretical and practical problems that are associated with work – particularly in the area of motivation – it cannot be said that they have received much encouragement to do so from either side of industry. The problem is that both management and workers have good reason to feel uneasy in the presence of psychologists and other behavioural scientists. Usually, psychologists are called in as consultants only when a firm is in trouble, so managers have come to regard the arrival of a psychologist on the premises as a sign that they are failing in their job. Trade union officials are even less pleased to find psychologists on the shop floor, not only because they remember the time and motion specialists – often psychologists – who used to make their lives a misery, but also because, however much the intruders may protest that they are looking for ways to make jobs more satisfying, the trade unionists are understand-ably reluctant to believe that anyone in the pay of management has the best interests of the workers at heart. Nor is either side re-assured by being told that behavioural scientists are seeking ways to eliminate conflict between them, since it is widely accepted in both management and union circles that such conflict is not only inevitable, but sometimes actually helpful. Outsiders are often shocked to hear such sentiments expressed, but we shall see later that this attitude, far from being defeatist, may actually incorporate an important principle of the art of industrial negotiation.

Industrial psychologists do not have an easy job, but they have been able to make a useful contribution to our under-standing of at least three important aspects of work. Perhaps their greatest achievement has been to pioneer many types of job enrichment scheme, often in the face of opposition from management and/or unions. Managements have had to be convinced that job enrichment makes economic sense, while many trade union officials believe it pointless to try and disguise the fact that certain types of job are necessarily unpleasant, and should simply be done as quickly, and for as much pay, as possible. Sometimes job enrichment involves reorganisation of the physical environment. For example, if telephonists are seated around a central console rather than along the walls of a room, they will find it easier to chat among themselves when they are not busy. Similarly, when workers are formed into groups instead of being isolated and independent units on an assembly line, they feel a greater responsibility, not only for their own task but for the work of the group. One effect of this change is to reduce absenteeism, since workers are less inclined to take a day off when they know the person who is going to be inconvenienced by their absence. And despite the reactions of the American automobile workers cited earlier, firms which employ these procedures are adamant that their workers prefer them to the conventional assembly line.

The psychological rationale behind job enrichment schemes is the attempt to get workers more involved in their jobs, and hence to exploit the basic human needs to be effective and to establish a satisfactory self-image. These needs can also be met by offering workers a greater say in how and when they should do their work, and even in the long-term planning of the firm. Unfortunately, worker participation schemes have been introduced in such a piecemeal fashion that it is very difficult to evaluate the effectiveness of the principle behind them. What is clear is that true *worker* participation commends itself to neither management nor unions, since both see it as a threat to their power and prestige – the more responsibility you give to individual members of the workforce, the less remains to be carved up between unions and management. Not surprisingly, closer inspection reveals that most worker participation schemes consist merely of a revision of existing consultation procedures between management and union officials, though a number of firms now have worker-directors, sometimes elected by the workforce but more commonly nominated by the unions. Surveys have generally found that workers who have experienced participation schemes value the opportunity to have a say in the organisation of their working lives – especially where matters of pay and safety are concerned – but it has also become apparent that schemes which just offer the workers a greater role in decision-making may cause more trouble than they prevent. The problem is a simple one: when workers are given a greater say in the running of the company in return for a promise to behave responsibly, they soon discover that 'behaving responsibly' is a euphemism for making sacrifices in order to safeguard the shareholders' profits. They have little incentive to accept these sacrifices, or to continue to participate in joint decision-making with management, unless they themselves are shareholders.

This suggests that worker participation schemes are unlikely to succeed in the long term, unless they offer workers not only an opportunity to contribute to the decision-making process and seats on the board, but also a financial stake in the company. In capitalist countries it is not easy to sell the complete participation package to either managements or unions, because the former are reluctant to share their traditional areas of responsibility, while the latter are not eager to share the consequences of lean years in a company's trading. And even where full participation is enforced by law, there is no guarantee that it will have the desired effect – a recent survey of workers' attitudes in different countries found that Yugoslavian factory workers, who owned the means of production and had the power of veto over their managers, felt that they had less influence over their immediate superiors than workers in comparable factories in America, where there were no formal worker participation programmes. International comparisons do, however, offer some support for the belief that participation makes economic sense: part of the reason for Italy's poor industrial record may lie in the fact that its factories still tend to be organised on rigidly hierarchical lines, with Italian managers being notoriously reluctant to delegate authority or to accept suggestions from below.

82

How to be a successful manager

The application of psychological principles to the art of management can help to make working a pleasanter and more productive occupation for all concerned. There are two important questions: how should a manager set about his job, and what sort of people make successful managers? So far as the first is concerned, a leading expert in the field has recently compressed the results of research into four rules of thumb which managers should follow. The first rule arises from evidence we have already considered: managers should look for ways of increasing the intrinsic attractiveness of jobs. While few firms can afford the massive reorganisation of job structure undertaken by the Swedish car giants, there are less expensive ways of improving the quality of working life by increasing the individual worker's autonomy and responsibility – for example, making the person who carries out a job also responsible for its inspection. But since some, especially older, workers don't want greater responsibility, job enrichment schemes should always be *offered* to the workforce, rather than imposed on it. It is also important to remember that people who are interested in increasing the intrinsic satisfaction of their jobs may be no less concerned with extrinsic satisfaction, so job enrichment should not be offered as an alternative to more pay. The second rule is to look for new incentives. We saw earlier that there is more to work motivation than money: giving workers greater autonomy in controlling their own work, and the 'job-and-finish' method, in which an agreed amount of work is carried out each day after which workers are free to go home, have both proved themselves to be effective motivators.

The third rule for managers is to find ways of creating a climate of openness and improved human relations. Irrespective of the political system in which it is operating, any firm will be an amalgam of groups whose interests cannot always coincide, so that some conflict is inevitable. Managers must therefore prepare themselves by studying the art of negotiation, but they should also realise that trouble can often be forestalled by ensuring that everyone receives a regular flow of information about what is going on in the company. Finally, even the best-intentioned schemes for improving the running of a firm are likely to founder if they are not planned in collaboration with the people whose lives they are supposed to enrich. Major reorganisations involving massive redundancies have been carried through with a minimum of conflict when representatives of all involved have been party to their planning, while quite minor changes have brought organisations to a halt when they have been imposed unilaterally by management. So remember that successful change requires participation.

The question of what makes a successful manager leads us into the area of personality and motivation. So far as male American managers are concerned, a recent study found that what distinguishes the successful (as measured by the sales record of their departments) from the unsuccessful is not their need for achievement, but the balance between their needs for power and for affiliation (the need to be liked): specifically, 80 per cent of the most successful departments investigated were found to be run by managers whose dominant need was for power, while 78 per cent of the less successful ones had managers whose power need was exceeded by the need for affiliation. The need for achievement, though known to be the dominant motivating force amongst successful entrepreneurs and innovators who set up their own businesses, did not distinguish between successful and unsuccessful managers. The reason why affiliative managers seem to fail is that their desire to be liked leads them to bend the rules to deal with an individual's problem, which violates one of the first principles of managing people – fairness. In attempting to gain the approval of one person they alienate others, and by seeming to make inconsistent decisions they destroy their subordinates' faith in the corporate reward system. This is why nice guys may make poor bosses.

But the finding that successful American managers have a strong need for power cannot be used to justify the old-fashioned, autocratic style of management. The need for power can take either of two distinct forms – personal or institutional – and individuals who seek personal power, who strive for dominance and tend to be rude and aggressive, rarely seek (and even more rarely achieve) institutional responsibility. Successful

American managers are found to be strongly inhibited about using power for their own ends; instead, they wield it to the greater glory of the company, and instil in those under them a sense of responsibility and a clear knowledge of the organisation. They stick to the rules, tend to favour a 'coach' rather than a 'dictator' style of management, and are prepared to sacrifice their own immediate self-interest when the interests of the organisation demand it. So in America it seems that 'company men', who can wield power without fear or favour, make the best managers. This may not necessarily apply in other countries, or where women managers are concerned. In Britain for example there is some evidence that, at the highest level of management, the need for achievement is more important than the need for power, though in their other major distinguishing characteristics – supervisory skill, initiative and involvement with their jobs (but not high intelligence) – top British managers seem closely to resemble their American colleagues. At present, we have too little information about the performance of women as managers to say whether they are more likely to succeed by adopting the behaviour of successful male managers, or by using some other style.

Striking a bargain

The art of industrial negotiation has been studied both by psychologists sitting in as observers on real industrial bargaining sessions, and also in the laboratory, where the effectiveness of different negotiating strategies can be compared by seeing how quickly each leads to the solution of a given problem. Thanks to these studies, we now know quite a lot about how negotiations ought to proceed, and why they often go wrong. The first principle is that both sides must recognise that there is a clash between their legitimate interests. Good negotiations begin with a thorough exploration of the conflict between the two sides, with positions being formally stated and vigorously defended against uncompromising criticism. This first stage serves two functions: it allows the negotiators to demonstrate to those whose interests they represent that justice has been done to their case, and also enables both sides to make an accurate assessment of the size of the problem and the strength of their opponents' case. It also establishes the extent to which both sides must be prepared to move from their predetermined positions, and any attempt to bypass it – for example, by either side making its 'final offer' at the very beginning of the negotiations – is likely to be counter-productive. The main threat to this crucial first stage of negotiation is that people who know each other socially and need to get on well in their everyday business tend to want to avoid unpleasantness. This so-called 'sweetheart relationship' is most marked in across-the-table negotiations between two people, when neither is willing to cause the other to lose face. It obstructs the negotiation process, because studies show that the more vigorous and frank the opening exchanges, the greater the likelihood that an equitable solution will be found. Where negotiation is concerned, there is strength in numbers; when circumstances dictate that each side has only a single representative, the evidence suggests that bargaining is best conducted over the telephone, because this reduces the possibility that either party will concede too much. Bear in mind that a successful negotiation leaves neither side feeling that it has lost.

Once the first stage is over, and the areas of conflict have been established, the negotiators can stop acting as representatives and contribute as individuals to the task of finding an acceptable route to the solution which may already be obvious to both sides. As time goes on, the negotiators become less competitive and more agreeable, and it becomes more difficult to tell which side they represent. If they know their business, the inter-party dispute of the first stage gives way to an inter-personal exchange of ideas; inexperienced negotiators, however, tend to cling to their initial aggressive posture, and the failure to progress to the inter-personal stage is a frequent cause of deadlock. This is particularly likely to occur when the two sets of negotiators don't know and have no reason to trust each other, so we can see that human relationships can obstruct negotiations in two opposite ways.

Another problem is that many negotiators fail to realise that a solution based on a straight compromise between the initial demands of the two sides may satisfy neither. The second stage of negotiation calls for imagination: ideal solutions usually involve the discovery of some new factor which allows both sides to achieve their full objectives – for example, a change in working procedures which increases productivity. Although there is no evidence that any particular personality character- istic – other than high intelligence – is linked with skill as a negotiator, women are found to be significantly better than men, not only at producing imaginative solutions, but more generally as negotiators. Ironically, they are grossly under- represented in both management and in senior positions in the trade union movement; although it is possible to train people to be more effective negotiators, the cause of smoother industrial relations would in all probability be better served by greatly increasing the involvement of women in the negotiation process.

Finally, international comparisons show that the art of industrial negotiation is better understood in some countries than in others. In North America and, to a lesser extent, Japan, there are a comparatively large number of strikes, but they tend to be brought to an end swiftly, as soon as agreement is reached on the broad outlines of a package of proposals. Northern Europeans, including the British, are much slower and more pedantic in their negotiations, and work is rarely resumed until each area of conflict has been resolved in detail. Satisfactory compromises are more common in North American negoti- ations, while a state of deadlock is reached more often in northern Europe (the position is rather different in southern Europe). As a result, strikes cost companies less in North America, so there is more money in the kitty to be haggled over. The relationship between management and unions tends to be closer in North America than in Europe (in America, the balance of power is also tilted much more in the favour of the former), so these differences may not reflect a significant difference in national characteristics. However, it is clear that Europeans, who tend to sneer at what they regard as a lack of sophistication in America's efforts at international diplomacy, have much to learn from her when it comes to domestic, industrial negotiations.

8 Buying

The fundamental questions about buying are what, why, who and where. What and why are, of course, interlinked questions: goods may be divided into durables and non-durables or into essentials and non-essentials, but the boundaries in both cases are so blurred that I am not convinced that either distinction is very useful. The designation of certain commodities as luxury goods for tax purposes will never gain universal assent, because different people have different views about what is essential, and so may the same person at different times in his life. Food is essential, but few people in industrialised countries would now regard as essential only those ingredients necessary for adequate nutrition, though they might be more prepared to do so during – say – a war. 'Essential' requirements change, and the basic need to stay alive and fit in wartime is overtaken by a desire for variety and stimulation during a period of peace and comparative prosperity. Food advertisers recognise this, which is why they try to convince us that a product is not only good for us (essential), but also a treat (non-essential), providing both a rational and an emotional incentive to buy it.

I mention advertising because it is impractical to discuss buying without at the same time considering selling: as buyers we are never free from the attentions of sellers and their henchmen the advertising and marketing men, who seek not only to understand and exploit our buying habits, but also to mould our purchasing behaviour. Stephen Leacock described advertising as the science of arresting the human intelligence long enough to get money from it. But the sellers don't have it all their own way; over the last twenty years or so, those who attempt to influence what we buy have had to change their tactics. They used to persuade us to buy only a particular brand or product, but the great mushrooming of products which has accompanied growing economic prosperity has forced them to adopt more subtle approaches. Brand loyalty has been exposed as a marketing myth – it is now acknowledged that even where we have a strong preference for a particular brand, we still like to flirt with rival products, especially when they are new. This aspect of purchasing behaviour is extremely robust, and may answer a basic need for variety. However, in the economic recession of the 1970s there are signs of a revival of campaigns designed to establish brand loyalty: only Persil mums are caring mums, and we can all spot the chap who drinks Guinness – he's the calm, relaxed one in the corner, content to wait for the head on his beer to subside. The techniques have become more sophisticated, but the aim of these campaigns is very long-standing.

The other major change in the tone of advertising campaigns in recent years has less flattering implications for us as buyers. In the 1950s and 1960s, advertisements were packed with information about the product, on the assumption that we decided what to buy on rational grounds; 'unique selling propositions' were brought to our attention, and our TV screens were filled with actors who exuded integrity as they made us offers no sensible person could possibly refuse. But surveys of people's voting habits carried out by sociologists have been seized on by admen as evidence that rational persuasion is wasted on us. The pollsters' pursuit of the floating voter has turned out to be something of a wild-goose chase. It now appears that most of us vote according to longstanding emotional loyalties, and only rarely change our minds in response to events. So advertisers, assuming that we buy as we vote, have tended to abandon campaigns which appeal to reason and calculation in favour of advertisements designed to play on our unconscious motivations and associations. It is difficult to evaluate the effectiveness of advertising (we don't know how well the product would have sold without advertisements), but the standard of qualitative market research – the investigation of our underlying motivation – is so poor, from a scientific point of view, that it is hard to believe in the picture sometimes conjured up of the consumer as a marionette who simply makes purchases according to the wishes of the omnipotent advertising and marketing men who pull the strings.

I am not of course denying that sellers try to persuade us to buy their goods, and to manipulate us by the use of clever marketing techniques such as the choice of colour for packaging material. Although colour associations vary from one person to the next, there are certain universal effects: for example, an object is judged to be larger when wrapped in a warm colour like red or yellow than when it is packed in blue or green. We also seem to have fixed ideas about the significance of certain colours for specific commodities. The same cup of coffee will be described in quite different terms, depending upon the colour of the tin it came from: coffee from a dark brown tin is judged to be strong; from a red tin, rich; from a blue tin, mild; from a yellow tin, weak. The manufacturer can't ignore these quirks of the potential customer, indeed he will seek to exploit them, but they present problems. Consider the plight of the designer who has to decide on the colour of a new cigarette pack – red is out because it suggests a harsh taste, green means menthol, brown reminds us of the farmyard, black is a sombre warning that we ought not to buy this or any other sort of cigarette, and pink may be too feminine. Ironically, although manufacturers devote so much thought to the packaging of their products, surveys make it clear that their efforts are not appreciated by consumers: according to a recent poll of British housewives' attitudes, their strongest feelings about packaging were worry that it added to the cost of goods (which of course it does), and fear that it was used to deceive them (which it sometimes is). They stated a strong preference for simple, transparent packaging wherever this is feasible.

Who buys what?

Traditionally, buyers were classified according to socio-economic status (SES), but the limitations for marketing purposes of this crude categorisation have become increasingly clear. We now know that the buying habits of, say, a single woman of twenty-four are markedly different from those of a married lady of the same SES and age: both may covet the same fur coat, but the enthusiasm of the latter is more likely to be dampened by the burden of mortgage repayments. The analysis of buying behaviour is now more sophisticated, and based on such psychological considerations as self-image, age, and peer and reference groups (sometimes these two coincide: for example, a fifteen-year-old boy may use Brut because he believes that other fifteen-year-olds do so, but sometimes they are different: fifteen-year-old boys used to apply Brylcreem to their hair because the advertisements told them that Denis Compton did so). The importance of self-image may be seen in the behaviour of people who buy cheap cigarettes to smoke at work but a more expensive brand for an evening out. It was exploited with a success which has become one of the legends of the British advertising world by Embassy cigarettes, which rose from nothing to being the leading brand in a highly competitive market on the strength of an advertising campaign which implied that anyone could smoke Embassy anywhere.

I said earlier that advertising and marketing techniques have become more sophisticated, but the effects of this are probably more than matched by the rise of the consumer movement. Studies show that the active pursuit of the best value for money is equally common at all levels of SES, though its motivation may differ: bargain-hunting may reflect the need to be economical, but it can also be a game. Price consciousness is a personality trait and as such is possessed by some people more than others, regardless of their economic circumstances. A recent Canadian study has pointed to a possible bone of contention between husbands and wives, arising from a difference in their attitude about value for money: although both partners were found to be equally concerned that the quality of an expensive consumer durable should justify its price before buying it, *after* the purchase had been made husbands tended to be significantly *less* satisfied than their wives that they had made a good buy.

Consumerism may have become a force to be reckoned with, but buyers have not had it all their own way. Sellers have fought back with a series of marketing manoeuvres designed to bamboozle all but the canniest shoppers. The abolition in Britain of retail price maintenance has encouraged the use of trading stamps, banded offers, 'special' offers (6p off – but off

91

what?), and the introduction of special-offer coupons. A number of studies have attempted to evaluate the effectiveness of these different techniques for persuading us to part with our money, and it appears that, in Britain, we are most attracted by the prospect of actually having cash handed back to us (a discount) when we have bought something.

Shopping

The pattern of who buys what is being altered, thanks to changes both in retailing procedures and in attitudes towards 'appropriate' sex roles. Traditionally, wives did all the household shopping, while their husbands bought cars and liquor and advised on major purchases like washing machines. A number of factors have combined to disrupt this pattern. It is now common for wives to make a major contribution to the family income and to have joint bank-accounts and credit cards. It is becoming accepted, especially among the under-forties, that the bulk of household shopping can be most conveniently accomplished on a weekend outing of the whole family to a supermarket – particularly when the mother works during the week.

Attitudes towards shopping have also been affected by the burgeoning of large chain stores, and there is no shortage of evidence about our views on the respective merits and demerits of shopping in large city-centre stores and local corner shops. Predictably, a study of a thousand residents in Watford found that in the city centre the shops themselves were the main attraction, whereas local stores were liked because they were familiar and provided an opportunity for meeting people and chatting, not only with other shoppers but with the shopkeepers whom they got to know. Shopping locally is also more reassuring; this may explain why many people prefer to buy patent medicines from their local chemist, although they could buy the same product more cheaply at a supermarket. More surprisingly, over half of the Watford sample said that the reassuring feeling of being in a familiar place was one reason why they enjoyed shopping in the town centre – which ought to please town planners, who are often criticised for the impersonality of shopping precincts. General reasons for enjoying shopping given in this survey included the feeling that it was something the respondents were good at as well as the opportunity it offered non-working women to get out and about. About half the sample said that they found household shopping enjoyable – but the survey was carried out in 1969, and there is some evidence that shopping is becoming less enjoyable, especially for working housewives who are forced to shop at the busiest times.

A more recent study has explored in detail our habits while on routine shopping expeditions. It confirms that most housewives do the bulk of their shopping during a weekly visit to the supermarket, and top up when necessary at the local store. The main expedition may be a weekend outing for the whole family, but there is also a trend towards late evening shopping on Thursday or Friday. Most housewives shop according to a fixed procedure: each week, they tend to go to the same store at the same time to buy similar goods, and closer observation shows that they also follow an identical route around the store on each occasion. Shopping lists seem to be a thing of the past, because the main function of such a list – to stop you forgetting vital items – has largely been made redundant by the fact that all the goods are on display in a supermarket. This may explain why shoppers like always to follow the same route around the store – they use its lay-out as a checklist. Nevertheless, the investigators found that, on average, shoppers tend to forget to make 10 per cent of the purchases they have planned, so lists may still serve a useful purpose.

I suspect that the real reason why people no longer use shopping lists is that they would make embarrassing reading when shoppers returned home, because the most striking fact which has emerged from detailed investigations of how we shop is that almost half the items we buy are goods we had no intention of purchasing when we entered the store! The reasons people give for making their unplanned purchases, when interviewed as they leave the store, are presented in the following chart:

Reasons for making unplanned purchases

Remembered it was needed	38%
Cheaper or on special offer	24%
A treat for self or children	17%
No reason	16%
Other reasons	4%
Bought instead of similar product	1%

Although all these purchases were unplanned, notice that only 16 per cent of them represent true *impulse buying*, which the shopper was unable to justify. Biscuits and cakes are the goods most likely to be bought on impulse (pet foods, tea and detergents are the least likely), and impulse buying is commoner amongst younger than older shoppers – though the total number of unplanned purchases is higher in the older age group, which suggests, surprisingly, that younger and less experienced shoppers may actually be better organised than their elders.

Observational studies have revealed another intriguing type of behaviour in supermarkets – *instinctive buying*. Because they have a regular route around the store, and also because they may be preoccupied with other matters, housewives make some purchases automatically, without regard to price. This is most marked in the early stages of the expedition, before they have warmed up. They stop their trolleys at a particular point, look around until something seems to click, pick up a product and then move on; when questioned afterwards, they have no recollection of their behaviour. An American study, in which shoppers were filmed and the rate at which they blinked was taken as a measure of their alertness, has also made the suggestion that very large stores have the effect of sending shoppers into a sort of trance. This effect can be enhanced by playing Musak, and it has also been found that the more goods there are on the shelves, the more likely it is that shoppers will enter this sleep-walking, trolley-filling state. A different American study has investigated the effect of varying the volume at which Musak is played: when it is played loud, shoppers buy the same amount but they shop faster. Since one of the most irritating aspects of supermarket shopping is being caught in a trolley jam in one section while the rest of the store is relatively empty, perhaps the day will come when we buy by (musical) numbers – divide a store up into sections, each with its own volume control, and the enterprising manager will be able to blast us out of vegetables or entice us to linger among the household cleaners, thus minimising our frustration while maximising his own profit!

It is in supermarkets that we find the slickest merchandising and the best thought-out attempts to manipulate what we buy, for example by the positioning of goods. To some extent, there is a 'natural order' governing the positions in which goods are displayed: we should be disturbed to find shoe polish next to butter, or spaghetti in among the soap powders. The location of some items will be dictated by the fear of contamination – soaps, being strong smelling, are kept away from dairy products – and others by consideration of the shopper's needs: for example, eggs and soft fruit tend to come towards the end of our route through the store, because they would be more likely to come to grief at the bottom of the basket. Special-offer bins are located at strategic points where we are likely to take a break (and make a quick, unplanned purchase), and the selection of items for display at the check-out point – sweets and cigarettes, for example – is designed to cater for the weary shopper's feeling that she deserves a reward. Sweets are doubly tempting here, both as self-indulgence and also as a means of rewarding a child who has been well behaved. Interestingly, studies show that housewives are well aware of the significance of these tempting goodies at the check-out queue, and take pleasure in beating the system by ignoring them (I wish I could say the same – I can rarely resist the razor blades). But special-offer racks in other parts of the store are very effective, especially when they contain damaged tins at knock-down prices. It is as if we have stumbled on them by chance, and we are only too prepared to take advantage of our good fortune. So although it may be true that we are becoming more accomplished at buying, it seems that the sellers still have a few tricks up their sleeves. That being so, here is a final tip to help you thwart them: whenever possible, go shopping for groceries *after*, and never immediately before, a meal – studies show that we spend significantly less when we shop just after we have eaten!

9 Remembering

Everyone complains of his memory, but no one complains of his judgement   Le Duc de la Rochefoucauld

What do we remember and how?

The short answer to this question is: more than you think, but probably not in the way you imagine. A wealth of evidence points to the conclusion that when our memories fail us, it is not that the information we wish to retrieve isn't there, but rather that we can't get access to it at that particular moment. Consider the *tip-of-the-tongue* phenomenon, that maddening feeling you have when you just can't quite remember, say, a name. You dredge up a host of other names, but the correct one continues to evade you. However, these other names are far from being a random assortment: when you are eventually reminded of the name you were after, you will find that it has some property in common with the list you have produced. They may all start with the same letter, or perhaps all have the same number of syllables. If the name you want is Wheatcroft, you may come up with Whitehouse, Whitlam or Wheatgerm; if it is Harman-Jones, maybe Owen-Smith, Marshall-Tones, or even Lycett-Green, will spring to mind. You may not be able to recall Wheatcroft or Harman-Jones, but it seems unlikely that you have actually forgotten the names, because they are clearly influencing the names you are producing.

Two other pieces of evidence make the same point. If you show British students a list of a couple of hundred place-names which include the names of all the states in the United States, they can usually pick out all the states' names without making any mistakes. But if, instead, you just ask them to write down the names of as many American states as they can remember, they will probably manage about thirty out of the fifty; and if, without warning them of your intention, you get them back a week later and make the same request, they will again produce about thirty names. But the interesting thing is that these will not be the same thirty, which suggests that somewhere in their memory they have the names of the great majority, if not all, of the states in the union, but that they can only recall a certain number at any given moment. Finally, suppose I were to ask you what you were doing on 10 December last year. Your initial reply would probably be that you hadn't the faintest idea. But if I made it worth your while, and gave you enough time, you might well be able to locate the day by referring to important events which occurred about that time, or by reconstructing your work schedule or your holiday arrangements, and surprise yourself by managing to recall quite a lot about the day.

These observations not only suggest that our memories are more fully stocked than we realise, but also tell us something about the way we remember things. Experimental psychologists have put forward two very different accounts of the process of remembering. According to the first, memory consists of a series of snapshots which we view whenever we wish to recall some past experience or item of information. If you ask how memories get laid down, exponents of this theory would say that we behave like the character in Christopher Isherwood's play who said: 'I am a camera with a shutter open, quite passive'. In essence, the theory describes both the laying-down and the recall of memories as passive and objective processes, and it is the view of memory presumably held by the people responsible for deciding what is admissible as evidence in a court of law, where great importance is attached to the recollection of eyewitnesses at the scene of a crime or an accident.

Unfortunately, it is now clear that this is not how memory works at all; moreover, it seems certain that the acceptance of what is known to be an erroneous view of the memory process is frequently responsible for miscarriages of justice. Consider the following experiments carried out by psychologists at the University of Washington, in Seattle. In the first, people watched a short film-clip of a lecture being disrupted by a group of demonstrators. They were then asked to complete one of two questionnaires about what they had seen, the one containing mildly-phrased questions ('Did you notice the demonstrators gesturing at any of the students in the class?' 'Did the professor say anything to the demonstrators?'), and the other having more aggressive phrasing ('Did you notice the militants threatening any of the students?' 'Did the professor shout something at the activists?'). A week later, the subjects were summoned back to answer a series of questions about the disruption they had watched: for example, was the incident quiet or noisy, peaceful or violent, pacifist or belligerent? The results were clear-cut: people who had answered the mildly-worded questionnaire the previous week remembered the disruption as being less noisy, violent and belligerent than those who had replied to the aggressively-worded questions immediately after seeing the film. They had all seen exactly the same events, but their recollection of them was clearly coloured by subtle forces at work while the scene was still fresh in their minds.

The same investigators have provided dramatic confirmation of this effect. In a later experiment, people were shown films of traffic accidents, and then asked to estimate the speed at which the vehicles involved had been travelling. The experimenters posed this question in one of five slightly different ways: some subjects were asked 'About how fast were the cars going when they hit each other?', while, in the other four phrasings, the word 'hit' was replaced by 'contacted', 'bumped into', 'collided with', or 'smashed into'. The graph opposite leaves little doubt that the alteration of a single word in the question had a significant effect on the average speed estimated. The average estimated speed produced by observers who were asked how fast the cars were travelling when they made contact with each other was less than 32 mph; those who had heard the evocative phrase 'smashed into' suggested an average speed of more than 40 mph. Nor is this all. A different group of subjects subsequently watched a film of a traffic accident, and were then asked either, 'About how fast were the cars going when they smashed into each other?' or, 'About how fast were the cars going when they hit each other?'; alternatively, some subjects were asked

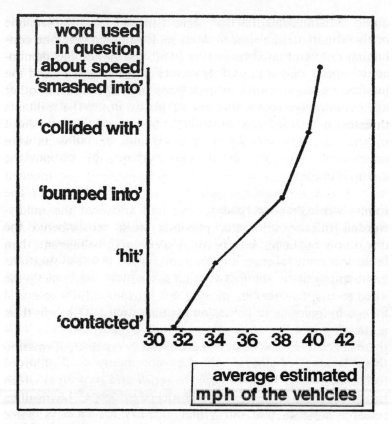

word used in question about speed	average estimated mph of the vehicles
'smashed into'	
'collided with'	
'bumped into'	
'hit'	
'contacted'	
	30 32 34 36 38 40 42

nothing at all about the speed of the cars. A week later, the observers were summoned back, and a further series of questions posed, including, 'Did you see any broken glass?' Twelve per cent of those who had been asked nothing about the speed of the cars the previous week, and 14 per cent of those who had answered the milder form of the question, said that they had seen broken glass, whereas 32 per cent of those who had been exposed to the question involving the words 'smashed into' said that they had noticed it. In actual fact, no broken glass had been shown in the film, so these results seem to provide overwhelming evidence against the view that our perception of events in any way resembles the action of a camera. They also make it clear that when we are remembering an event, we actively reconstruct it rather than passively watching a 'film' made at the time of its occurrence. We may have reservations about the statement that the camera cannot lie, but it is palpably false to make a similar claim for the human eye. Research has also shown that there is very little connection between the actual speed of a car and observers' estimates of it, so the implication seems plain: it is pointless (and often misleading) to ask eyewitnesses to an accident to testify in court about car speeds, since their answers could be so powerfully influenced by the way in which the question is put, by police officers immediately after the event and, perhaps, by prosecuting counsels in court.

Psychology in the court room

But this isn't the only respect in which our knowledge about the workings of memory suggests that law-court procedures are at fault. In a criminal case, it is common for the prosecution to lay great emphasis on the fact that an eyewitness has later recognised a suspect, either by picking out his photograph in police files or by pointing to him at an identification parade, when he is standing in a line of people who look roughly alike. In both these procedures, the witnesses are asked to *recognise* a suspect; there is also, of course, the less commonly used photofit technique, which requires them to *recall* and *reconstruct* what he looks like. How reliable is this sort of evidence? Laboratory research suggests that our visual memory for faces is pretty impressive: if you show people a series of pictures of faces, and the next day present them with pairs of photographs – one previously seen, the other not – nine times out of ten they are able to identify the face they have seen before. And if you show them pictures of *objects*, they can identify them with a similar degree of accuracy even after looking at a staggering total of 10,000 pictures over the previous five days! Such findings might suggest that eyewitness testimony ought to be treated as powerful evidence, but the trouble is that in real life we don't reproduce our laboratory efficiency, especially when we have witnessed a crime.

There are many reasons for this. As a laboratory subject, you are usually given five or ten seconds to peruse a picture; at the scene of a crime, you may catch only a brief glimpse of the criminal's face. More importantly, in the laboratory you are relaxed and have been instructed to concentrate on memorising the faces, whereas if you are in a bank which is being robbed, you may well be mesmerised by fear and shock; if you are capable of rational thought at all, you're more likely to devote it to figuring out how to prevent the gunman from shooting you than to coolly memorising his face. Moreover, there is evidence that fear and stress cause us to abandon the sophisticated techniques we normally use when looking at faces in favour of a more primitive and prejudiced type of thinking, in which we rely heavily on stereotypes of the sort we shall be discussing in the next chapter. Despite the cherubic appearance of some of history's nastiest murderers, we all have a crude idea about what criminals ought to look like (they are scarred and have cauliflower ears), and it is much more common for people who have witnessed a violent crime to describe the villain as 'fierce looking' than to comment on the colour of his hair, the shape of his nose or other distinctive features. Of course, if this is what they have noticed, their task at a subsequent identification parade will be made more difficult: the suspect may not be able to change the colour of his hair or the shape of his nose, but he will certainly be careful to avoid the frightening expression he assumed at the time of the crime to intimidate the bank clerks. What is more, examination of police records reveals that the more emotion-provoking a crime is, the less well people remember it: witnesses' descriptions are more accurate after a robbery, for example, than after a rape or assault. So the fact that we are good at recognising faces in the laboratory is irrelevant to the question of how much significance should be attached to eyewitness evidence in court: witnesses to a crime form impressions under great stress, and it is doubtful whether either a police station or a criminal court is the ideal place in which to retrieve such memories as they have.

There is no shortage of cases in which it has subsequently been found that identification parades have led to the conviction of an innocent person. Unfortunately, the rules which govern this procedure, although drawn up with the aim of eliminating inaccurate identification, may actually have the opposite effect. For example, placing a suspect amongst others of similar appearance is likely just to confuse the witness, since

101

all the evidence shows that these are precisely the circumstances in which we are *least* good at recognising a face we have seen before. Moreover, allowing a suspect to choose his position in the line may also lead to trouble, since any professional criminal knows that the further down the line he stands, the less likely he is to be identified. Another problem is that, in the present procedure, the witness knows that *someone* in the line is supposed to be guilty, which makes his task more an exercise in assessing which of the people he is inspecting is most likely to be guilty than one of simple recognition. This of course will encourage him to fall back on his stereotypes about what criminals look like. One way of getting around this problem – proposed by the police – might be to require each witness to attend two different identification parades, having been told that the suspect was in only one of them. But even here, there would be pressures on the witness to identify somebody in the second parade if he had failed to do so in the first. The effect of all these confusing factors may be further compounded by the nature of what the witness is actually being asked to do: social convention is strongly opposed to us staring at people, so the *embarrassment* of an identification parade may well disturb the witness's ability to perform his task, and perhaps lead to premature identification.

Many of these disturbing and embarrassing factors can be eliminated by confronting witnesses not with real people, but with photographs of them, and an experiment carried out recently by psychologists at Nottingham University suggests that this might be a more reliable procedure. Subjects were shown a short colour film of an office break-in, in which the criminal was seen clearly for ten seconds; a week later, half of them attended a mock identification parade, run according to police procedures, while the rest tried to identify the criminal from colour slides, which showed three different views of each of the nine men in the identification parade. There were significantly more correct identifications, and less incorrect ones, by those who had seen slides than by those attending the identification parade. At the parade, only ten of the thirty-five witnesses felt able to make a positive identification, and five of these were actually incorrect. Even when the slides were used, there were only nine correct positive identifications – which suggests that our visual memories may be rather less impressive than the results of the studies discussed at the beginning of this section indicated.

So far, we have seen that the eyewitness testimony of the man in the street is a flimsy foundation on which to base a criminal prosecution. But remembering faces is a skill which the police consider can be improved. Trainee policemen are taught that the easiest and most useful features of a face to note and remember – especially if you get no more than a brief glance – are, first, the shape of the upper head and the style and colour of the hair, and, secondly, the facial outline – cheek, jaw and chin. (Unfortunately, what witnesses usually remember are the features of the central corridor of a face – eyes, nose and mouth – which tend to attract emotional labels and also to be fairly mobile, both of which makes them hard to recall accurately.) But are the police, who have been trained to observe scientifically under conditions of stress, any more reliable as eyewitnesses than the rest of us? The case of George Davis, who was convicted after being picked out of an identity parade by five policemen when thirty-eight other witnesses failed to recognise him, but subsequently found to be innocent, inspires little confidence that their training affects their ability to recognise a face.

Laboratory studies which have compared policemen's powers of observation and memory with those of members of the general public do nothing to allay these doubts. So far as the basic capacity to recall units of information is concerned, policemen turn out to be nothing special: like anyone else, they find it difficult to commit more than six or seven items of information to memory – it is, of course, no accident that neither telephone nor car registration numbers exceed the magic number of seven digits. But surely their training makes policemen expert at perceiving events and people? Let us consider the evidence for this comforting belief. In one experiment, researchers at the Applied Psychology Unit in Cambridge showed films of a street-scene lasting several hours to a group of civilians and policemen, who were instructed to watch out for certain target people and various kinds of action – theft and

103

other forms of antisocial behaviour – which had been inserted into the film. After viewing it, the police officers made more *allegations* of theft than the civilians, but were found to be no better at spotting *actual* offences. Incidentally, the overall detection rate in both groups was a mere 31 per cent, despite the fact that photographs of the target people were displayed next to the screen during the film; even when the observers were 'primed', by being shown a film of the people they were supposed to be looking for, more than half the events they had been told to look out for passed undetected.

Other studies, both British and American, confirm that the main difference between police and civilian observers is the greater tendency of the former to notice and recall sinister events which have not actually happened. In one experiment, New York policemen and civilian observers watched a 42-second film in which a man approached a pram, pulled down its protective net, and then walked off. As he did so, a woman came out of an adjacent house. End of film. The observers made statements about what they had seen immediately afterwards, and a week later. The most striking result of this study was that although the police managed to recall more correct details about the dress and appearance of the protagonists immediately after they had seen the film, they also reported twice as many *incorrect* 'facts' as the civilians a week later: for example, one in every five policemen said that he had seen the man reach into the pram and remove a baby!

In a similar American study, policemen and members of the public watched a sequence of street-scenes on film, and were later asked about both details of the scenes and the possible intentions of the actors involved. Here, there was no difference between the two groups in their ability to recall objective details, but once again the police reported significantly more 'criminal episodes'. For example, a man who walked round a corner carrying a can was seen by non-police observers as having run out of petrol, whereas a majority of the policemen assumed that he was an arsonist.

All in all, then, it looks as if the police are little better at perceiving and remembering events and people than the rest of us; what is more, perhaps because of their past experience, they are particularly prone to misinterpret events. Policemen are paid to have suspicious minds, but I find it rather disturbing that the testimony which they give in court, weeks after they have seen a crime being committed, is likely to be even *less* reliable than similar evidence from a member of the general public. Moreover, length of service in the force, which is frequently referred to in court as adding weight to the evidence of a police eyewitness, actually seems to be irrelevant. According to the results of a recent British study, neither the age nor the experience of a policeman is related to his ability to identify people in photographs. It seems likely that any advantage that experience brings to his powers of observation and memory is cancelled out, because he may have become less open-minded, with stereotyped attitudes, prejudices and expectations.

Improving your memory

We have seen that in some respects our memories may be more efficient than we realise, although, in certain circumstances, our confidence in people's recollection of events and faces is probably ill-founded. But most of us have the feeling that we should get further if only we had a better memory. Actually, people probably worry unnecessarily about their ability to remember things, because remembering seems to be an accomplishment of declining importance, and has been ever since the invention of the printing press. In earlier times, we had to rely on our memory for storing information and preserving our culture. This *oral tradition* still survives in some parts of the world – in Alex Haley's best-selling book *Roots*, the protagonist returns to Africa to explore his origins, and finds a man who still carries four hundred years of the tribe's history in his head. But most of us no longer need to remember more than *where* we can find information when we need to use it. Increasingly we are turning to *external* memory systems: our offices are full of reference books and card-index systems which free us from the necessity of carrying facts and figures in our heads, and modern educational practice recognises this by encouraging children to think *about* things, rather than insisting that they spend their time committing to memory information which they could simply look up in books. As Cardinal Newman observed, a great memory doesn't make a mind any more than a dictionary is a piece of literature.

Of course, most examinations still make demands on memory, but their structure is such that we only have time to display a fraction of the knowledge to which we have been exposed. It may be at examination time that we complain most bitterly about our memories, but the limitations of memory may actually be a blessing in disguise when we have only forty-five minutes to show what we know about a subject. It seems more likely that people who do poorly in examinations do so either because they find the situation too stressful, or because they have failed to organise their knowledge properly before the examination and remembered the wrong things.

It may be useful to remember *how* to do things, like changing a tyre between one puncture and the next, and also to be able to remember items of information on a very short-term basis, so that we can for example dial a phone number we have just been given, or read to the end of a long sentence without forgetting what was said at the beginning. But children are unlikely to thank us for making them memorise lists of formulae, the dates of English monarchs, or even pages of Shakespeare, unless they subsequently find themselves deprived of books – as prisoners of war, for example – or become addicted to cross-word puzzles or games like chess and bridge. I believe we are approaching the time when a 'good' memory will be appreciated as a party-trick or an aid to playing games or solving puzzles, but will not be especially valuable in our everyday business or domestic routine. It is interesting to note that people with freakishly good memories, who have been intensively studied by psychologists, very often complain that their perfect memory makes it impossible for them to lead a normal or happy life, and say that they would willingly trade in their memory for a more flawed model!

Aides-mémoire
What are the factors which help you to remember things in the normal course of events, and are there special tricks you can learn to improve your memory? There is convincing evidence that things are remembered best in the environment in which

they were learned – a fact tacitly assumed by crime novelists such as Wilkie Collins, whose detective brought people back to the scene of the crime to jog their memories, long before experimental psychologists demonstrated it in their laboratories. We know that if divers are made to learn lists of unrelated words while they are under water, they subsequently recall more of the words underwater than on dry land. Not only where but *when* we learn a thing may affect how well we remember it. Due to the body's biological rhythms, we are more alert in the morning than in the afternoon. But very recently it has been shown that if children are read a story at 9 a.m. and then tested a week later to see how much they remember about it, they recall significantly *less* than if they are read the story at 3 p.m. Being too alert may actually mean that we lay down less information in our long-term memory stores, so we may well have to rethink our ideas about the organisation of children's and students' timetables. Closely related to this is the phenomenon of *state-dependency*: when we learn something under the influence of a drug, it is recalled best when we are in the same physiological state. Here, laboratory studies support the observations of clinicians that heavy drinkers, when sober, are unable to find bottles and money they have hidden when drunk, but remember their hiding-places when once again drunk.

There is also evidence that being highly aroused (in an exam, for example) helps us to recall familiar facts, but makes it more difficult to recall more recondite information, an effect which is most marked in people who are by nature introverted. The popular belief that recall is better after a period of sleep than after wakefulness also seems to be well founded, though it is not clear why. Since depriving people of sleep does not impair their early morning recall, it may just be a reflection of our body-rhythms. It has also been suggested that smoking improves our ability to remember, but this is still conjecture: nicotine has been shown to improve rats' capacity to learn and remember things, but this has not yet been unambiguously demonstrated in people.

Finally, we come to *mnemonics*, schemes which help us to remember things we might otherwise forget. Most of these systems involve either a reduction or an elaboration of the way we encode information. In the former, we strip away irrelevant information in order to have as little as possible to remember. You might for example use the acronym ROYGBIV to remember the order of the colours of the spectrum (red, orange, yellow, green, blue, indigo, violet), or tie a knot in your handkerchief to remind you to go to the chemist. But you may have great difficulty in decoding the mnemonic you have so carefully constructed: you may remember ROYGBIV, but do you remember what the letter 'I' stands for? And what on earth is that knot in your handkerchief supposed to remind you to do?

Most mnemonic systems involve elaboration of the information to be stored, either verbally or – more commonly – by using visual images. One classic technique is the method of *loci*, where you first memorise a sequence of locations – for example, the rooms and cupboards in your house – and then visualise each of the items in a list which you have to remember sitting in one of these locations. So if you have a long shopping list beginning with eggs, sausages and potatoes, you could start to memorise it by imagining your bedroom full of eggs, a pile of sausages in your wardrobe, and potatoes in the laundry-basket. Alternatively, you could use the number-peg mnemonic, in which numbers are associated with a rhyming object (one-bun, two-shoe, three-tree), and you picture the items you want to remember in relation to the relevant peg-word: an egg on a bun, a shoe full of sausages, potatoes growing on a tree, and so on.

My objection to such systems is not that they don't work – they do, and can usefully be adapted to help with tasks like learning the vocabulary of a foreign language – but simply that I don't see their necessity. If I want to remember what to buy in the market, I write out a shopping list. The last thing I want to do is to clutter up valuable (and, in my case, painfully limited) memory capacity with unnecessary images of shoes full of sausages: they might disturb the equally inessential, but much more interesting, information I am struggling to preserve, such as the recipe for gin fizz and the names of the musicians who have played in Duke Ellington's bands over the last fifty years. Before the advent of printing and general literacy, mnemonic systems were useful because memory itself was so much more important. Orators in Ancient Greece used them, for example, because they had to memorise their speeches. But the modern politician who rises to his feet without written notes is a rare figure, and this change is symbolic of the fact that the ability to remember in detail is no longer a necessary or particularly admirable accomplishment.

10 Judging

In the last chapter I suggested that our knowledge of the workings of human memory may cause us to have grave misgivings about the weight which courts of law at present attach to evidence given by eyewitnesses to a crime. Unfortunately, this is not the only respect in which psychologists' findings can make us uneasy about the judicial process. Let us begin by looking at some experiments which throw light upon what goes on during the final, crucial stages of a trial, when the jury has to make a judgement on which the fate of the accused rests.

Twelve just men

In theory, the job of a trial jury is to listen to all the evidence presented, form impressions of the various parties involved (including the accused), and then to reach a verdict based on an objective assessment of what they have heard and seen. It is assumed that a decision made by twelve people is preferable to one made by a single individual, since individual prejudices and biases can be exposed in discussion, thus allowing a verdict to be reached on purely rational consideration of the facts. For what actually goes on in the jury room at a real trial, we have to rely on anecdote and conjecture; since the presence of psychologists would be unlikely to make the jurors' task any easier, it is quite right that they should not be allowed to sit in on the discussions. We do, however, have indirect evidence about the way in which juries reach their verdicts, from studies in which the tape-recorded transcripts of real trials are played to 'juries' recruited from the general public (as real jurors are), who can be observed, and even exposed to experimental manipulation, while trying to arrive at a decision.

I doubt if you will be surprised to learn that the most striking finding to emerge from these studies is that we are no more objective at judging than we are at remembering. In one experiment, subjects were asked to re-enact the role of a jury at a civil law case, in which they had to assess the sum to be paid in damages to a farm-worker who had badly cut his hand on improperly maintained farm equipment. The task was carried out by a number of different 'juries', and it was found that the level of damages they awarded could be greatly inflated by the simple expedient of showing a picture of the damaged hand while the jurors listened to details of the accident. This brings to mind the celebrated case of a Boston doctor accused of man-slaughter after performing an abortion, in which photographs of the aborted foetus were allowed to be shown as evidence. The pictures could have played no part in helping the jury to estab-lish the facts of the case; indeed, the practice of allowing juries to examine murder weapons or photographs of mutilated bodies can only make it less likely that they will reach their verdict on rational grounds.

Even when they are not encouraged to react emotionally by manipulative prosecutors, juries may be less influenced by the evidence presented than by the subjective impressions they form about the protagonists, and we shall see that these impressions may be creatures of little substance. Moreover, whereas in theft trials jurors' attitudes towards the defendant are found to change as the evidence unfolds, in rape trials jurors show a worrying tendency to stick to their initial impressions – and, in these trials, it is their attitude towards the victim rather than the defendant which turns out to be the single most important factor in determining the verdict they reach at the end of the day. Trial re-enactment studies reveal that juries are particu-larly influenced by their assessment of character in five key areas – how friendly, warm, trustworthy, competent and in-telligent a person appears. In a case of theft, if the defendant strikes them as untrustworthy and stupid, they initially see him as guilty; in discussions at the end of the trial, his intelligence becomes a less important factor, though their judgement of his trustworthiness – reasonably enough – influences their verdict. But in a rape case, if the jurors consider the *victim* untrust-worthy, the defendant is likely to get off, regardless of the impression he creates or the nature of his defence.

I repeat that this evidence comes from mock trials, and that we cannot assume that real-life jurors have an equally scanty regard for the evidence they hear. But the fact that subjective impressions are so important even when the 'jurors' can't see the witnesses (they are usually just listening to a tape-recording of the court proceedings), coupled with the finding that people in groups tend to take riskier decisions than they would as individuals (probably because they feel less responsibility for any consequences their decisions may have), suggests that the effectiveness of the jury system might at least bear empirical examination.

Making assessments

In everyday life we are continually having to make judgements about other people and their intentions. These may be snap decisions – is the motorist approaching my car really angry enough to thump me for denting his bumper? – or they may reflect a considered judgement: on balance, I think that the brash young man I have just been talking to is less likely to make a success of a university psychology course than the nervous, but more thoughtful, person I interviewed this morning. Both these examples show how important it is to be able to make accurate assessments: in the first case, my nose is at stake; in the second, the future careers of two school leavers are in the balance. But I chose these instances to illustrate the distinction between two different sorts of judgement we make when assessing others. Not only do we need to be able to assess people's current mood, on the basis both of their overt behaviour and more subtle cues about their intentions (is the affronted car-owner rolling up his sleeves for violent action, or is he just trying to look at his watch?), but we also often have to decide what sort of people *in general* they are.

How do we perceive others? Is judgement a skill we are born with, or do we have to learn it? If the latter, can people who are poor judges benefit from special training in this most important of social skills? In at least one respect, our ability to form impressions about other people seems to be innate. In the chapter on smiling I mentioned Paul Ekman's finding that the expression and interpretation of simple emotional states (happiness, fear, anger, and so forth) is similar in a wide variety of cultures. But Ekman's method was to ask people to identify emotions from pictures of actors who had been instructed to assume the appropriate expression, and a moment's thought shows that this procedure has very little in common with the circumstances in which we have to judge other people's feelings in everyday life. Few of the people we deal with are obliging enough to assume the snarling, contorted expression of Ekman's actors when they are angry, and we should be ill-advised to take the cheery smile of the man who is trying to sell us a car as an indication either that he is deliriously happy, or that he wishes us well.

Most of our assessments reflect a series of inferences based on past experience (in this respect, our perception of people is like our perception of anything else), and the use of analogy with our own behaviour and feelings – which is why, as we shall see later, we are best at judging people who are like us. Given the sophistication of the process, it isn't surprising that the ability to judge others is an acquired skill, and one which can be improved with training. The inference rules we use when forming opinions about others take the form of syllogisms. For example: all good-looking men are vain (past experience, and our reading of women's magazines, tells us so); the man in front of us is good-looking (current observation); therefore he is vain (preliminary judgement). We have at our disposal a system of pigeonholes which contain clusters of individual attributes which generally seem, on past experience, to go together. Each pigeonhole has one or more key attributes which enables us to place a new person in the appropriate slot. The procedure is not, of course, consciously formulated, and its main drawback is that it assumes a consistency which isn't always justified – not all small men are pushy, nor all fat people jolly – but using stereotypes is probably the most efficient way of beginning the process of appraisal. The good judge of people treats a preliminary classification as no more than an hypothesis which may have to be revised in the light of later information. The bigot, on the other hand, fits person to stereotype once and for all, and simply ignores subsequent evidence of miscasting, in the same way as he disregards evidence which contradicts any of his other beliefs. To take an extreme example, it is most unlikely that the flat-earther who dismisses photographs taken from outer space as faked material for a government propaganda campaign will have the mental flexibility to be a good judge of character, except possibly of like-minded individuals.

Within a culture there seems to be widespread agreement about what characteristics we expect to go together, and also about the broad categories of people which fit them. For example, ethnic stereotypes – Turks are cruel, Germans efficient, Jews clever – are still quite powerful, although there is some evidence that their influence is declining. When trying to refine our preliminary assessment of someone we want to judge we of course pay close attention to what they say, but there are plenty of physical cues by which we start to form an impression, long before they open their mouths. We examine a person's face, physique, clothes and hairstyle, and listen to the tone and accent of his voice, irrespective of the content of his remarks. Below are some examples of the inferences which social psychologists have found are commonly made from

Physical clues to character	
Sallow complexion	= hostility
Blond hair	= goodness and virtue
Wrinkles around eyes	= good humour and friendliness
Old age	= maturity and wisdom
Glasses/high forehead	= intelligence
(*in women*)	
Thick lips	= sexiness
Thin lips	= unsexiness
Bowed lips	= conceit, immorality, a demanding nature

physical appearance in North America: some of them apply in other cultures, others do not. Some of these inferences are supported by empirical testing: for example, short-sighted people *do* on average tend to have higher I.Q. scores than those with normal sight. But many of the inferences we make reflect irrational biases, the tendency to project our own values on to others, or the application of rules we have devised as a defence mechanism to protect us after a series of traumatic experiences – for example, after a number of disastrous love affairs, a man may decide that all women are untrustworthy, and this will colour his judgement of any woman he meets subsequently.

Many factors deflect us from making accurate, objective assessments of other people. Our judgements are subject to *halo-effects*: if we are struck by a single positive aspect of a person, we tend to exaggerate his excellence in other respects, instead of assessing each quality independently. For example, our judgements are known to be biased in favour of physically attractive individuals: as if they didn't already have enough going for them, good-looking children are judged by their teachers to be more intelligent than their less personable class-mates, while handsome defendants get off with significantly lighter sentences in mock trials (though not when the charge is fraud, which suggests that we take a dim view of people who exploit their good looks for criminal purposes!). So far as the clothes and hairstyle of a person being judged are concerned, the important thing is that they should conform to those of the assessor: a 'respectable' appearance may be more likely to persuade a middle-class commuter to answer a questionnaire you are brandishing, but less likely to attract signatures from students for an anti-war petition (these are both empirical findings). The fact that physical appearance can have such an effect illustrates the disproportionate importance of first impressions on the result of a judgement; it is worth remembering that it appears to be extremely difficult to improve on the impression you create during the first three minutes of an interview, however long it continues subsequently.

Our judgements also seem to be distorted by a *primacy effect*: a number of experimenters have shown that if you ask people to make an assessment of someone they have never met but have heard described by a list of adjectives, their judgements will be more strongly determined by the adjectives at the beginning of the list than by those which come later – a favourable or unfavourable impression is created by whatever they hear first, and it seems likely that a similar thing happens in real-life interviews. We also make simple logical errors when assessing people: for example, we may assume that a high level of energy implies that a person must be aggressive. Finally, although I said earlier that we function most reliably as interviewers when we are trying to assess people who are similar to ourselves, there is some evidence that, in our everyday lives, we make a deeper analysis of the character of people we *dis*like. This may be because we are more often called upon to justify our dislikes than our likes or, alternatively, because we tend to follow Marx's dictum, Get to know your enemy, so that we can attack him (and resist his attacks) more effectively.

What makes a good judge?

It is widely accepted that some of us are better judges of people than others. But this has proved a difficult proposition to test experimentally because it is not at all easy to gauge the accuracy of such assessments; after all, who is to say what the person being judged is *really* like? Real-life settings pose an additional problem: the ideal way to test the efficiency of an interviewer would be to make a note of his selections, but actually accept all the candidates he has interviewed, and then see whether the people he recommended turn out to be more successful than those he advised against. Unfortunately – though understandably – firms and institutions don't queue up for the privilege of taking part in this sort of investigation, so we are obliged to use less direct methods to assess people's ability to assess.

Contrary to common belief, women do not in general seem to be better judges of character than men, though they are more inclined to use psychological terms in their assessments, whereas men (like children) tend to make appraisals more in terms of achievements or physical characteristics. There are other differences between the sexes: while men who are good at judging other men are found also to be good at assessing women, women who are good judges of their own sex tend to be rather unreliable when called upon to assess men. Sex differences cloud the issue when we try to establish what sort of people make good judges, because there seems to be a complex interaction between the personality of the assessor, his or her skill at judging people, and the sex of both the assessor and the

116

person being assessed. Specifically, men who are good at judging other men tend to be dominant, outgoing, aggressive and tactless, whereas those who are most accurate in their opinions about women are tolerant, tactful, and – in other respects – rather ineffectual. The best female judges of the male character are found to be submissive, reasonable and accepting, while women who are best at assessing other women tend to be inhibited, insecure and physically unattractive. These results are rather unexpected, but they have been confirmed in several studies; however, they apply only to the accuracy of first impressions, and it must be pointed out that the studies used only American subjects. They suggest that there is no simple connection between personality and the ability to judge people, and also make it clear that the good judge of character will not necessarily be a socially polished individual. The picture is further complicated by the fact that the ability to judge doesn't seem to be a single skill: the evidence suggests that people acquire highly specific skills at recognising certain qualities in other people, rather than an overall ability to become good at judging.

Do interviews work?

We have discussed some of the factors which influence the way in which we form opinions about other people in everyday life, and have also seen how easy it is to warp the judgements of jurors in a court of law. I shall now myself pass judgement on the effectiveness of the formal procedure in which we most commonly find ourselves judging or being judged in our professional lives – the interview. There are three main types of interview: the one-to-one conversation, the board interview (where a panel of interviewers puts questions to a single candidate), and the group assessment (in which a group of candidates are observed by one or more assessors, while having a discussion or working together to solve some problem). We shall see that each method has its strengths and weaknesses, but that none of them inspires much confidence as a method of selection on its own.

The one-to-one interview is used most commonly, and has the obvious advantage of being more like ordinary conversation. Provided the interviewer knows his business, the candidate should feel tolerably at ease and be able to answer questions naturally and fully. The interviewer can learn a good deal about the candidate and, after it, will be in a position to make a well-informed guess as to whether he personally would enjoy working with the candidate, and how well the candidate would fit into the organisation as a whole. The drawback of this comparatively intimate procedure is that the interviewer's personal feelings about the candidate may distort his judgement of the latter's real qualities; there is also a danger that the two will strike up such a good relationship that the interview will degenerate into a chat about mutual interests. For this reason, it is unwise ever to make a selection on the basis of a single one-to-one interview.

The board interview has the advantage that it seems fairer to the candidate (though he may find it a more intimidating procedure), and also that it brings out the best in interviewers; since they are being observed by their colleagues, they are more likely to stick to the business in hand, and the interview is less likely to wander off into irrelevancies. However, the candidate is never allowed to forget that he is being assessed, so that his answers will be contrived and unlikely to reveal much of his true personality. He may also be put off by having to switch from one conversation to another, as different interviewers pose their questions. Board interviews can reduce the effect of individual bias (though a powerful chairman may still manage to impose his prejudices on the eventual choice between candidates), but they are unlikely to produce much useful information about what the candidate will be like under normal working conditions. They operate in favour of people who respond well to stress, and are therefore most effective when candidates are being selected for jobs where working conditions actually are stressful. Remember, too, that groups make more irresponsible decisions than individuals, since no one member feels that he will have to carry the can for the decision, so there is no guarantee that boards will make more reliable judgements than interviewers who have had one-to-one conversations with the candidates.

Group interviews are a fairly recent development. The 'interviewer' sets a problem or provides a topic for discussion, and then just sits back and watches how the candidates behave. The advantages of this procedure are that the situation is fairly lifelike, so the candidates will behave naturally, and that the interviewer, freed from the obligation to think up questions, is likely to be more accurate in his observations. The main difficulty is that a single aggressive individual can dominate the proceedings and cause all the other candidates to give up. Moreover, we only learn how people will behave in a group; for many jobs, it may be more important to know how a candidate will work on his own, or under a particular boss.

The question of how effective the various types of interview are is not an easy one to answer: as I pointed out earlier, real interviews tend to have too much practical importance for psychologists to be able to evaluate their effectiveness in the ideal manner. Such studies as there are have shown that different members of a board are more likely to agree in their judgements than interviewers who have conducted independent one-to-one conversations with a candidate, but this is hardly surprising – after all, members of a panel are making their judgements on the basis of identical evidence, while individual interviewers will each have elicited different information from the candidate. Nor does the unanimity of members of a board mean that they have made a wise choice: they may simply be agreed on a wrong decision. In fact, there is no evidence that the selection process is made more reliable by the inclusion of any sort of interview. If we possess written biographical information about a candidate, and know how well he has performed at some objective test designed to assess proficiency at whatever it is that he is applying to do, the accuracy of our prediction about how well he will make out is not significantly improved by interviewing him.

However, this does not imply that interviews serve no useful purpose. Where a prospective employee is going to work under a particular boss or as part of an interdependent team, one-to-one and group interviews may play an important role in the selection process. Moreover, the one-to-one interview can be a convenient vehicle for conveying information to the candidate about the organisation he has applied to join, because it is not only the candidate who is being judged at an interview. The interviewer may be trying to decide on the best candidate for the job, but the candidates are also trying to make a decision: would they enjoy working for the organisation, if they were offered the job? One-to-one interviews give the interviewer an opportunity to sell the organisation and himself to people whom he wants not only to assess, but also to impress.

Tips for interviewers

The scientific investigation of interviews may present a gloomy picture of their effectiveness as a means of selection, but it has pointed to a number of ways in which an interviewer can improve his technique. Since we show no sign of abandoning the practice of interviewing, we may as well perform the task as efficiently as possible. On the basis of research findings a number of recommendations can be made as to how best to achieve certain objectives, which any experienced interviewer will recognise. First, you may want to get the candidate to talk more. Relaxed conversation seems to be encouraged by placing the chairs a comfortable distance apart, at an angle of between 90 and 120 degrees, and you should not be seated behind a desk (these matters were discussed in Chapter 1). You should look the candidate in the eye, and smile as he finishes a question; you should also be prepared to talk about yourself and give your own views, and should neither interrupt the candidate nor allow long pauses in the conversation. Secondly, you may wish to get the candidate to enlarge on a topic, which you can do either by making encouraging noises or by expressing mild disagreement with what has been said. Thirdly, if you want to change the subject or stop the candidate talking, either express firm agreement and look away from him, or sit forward, ostentatiously moving your arms further in front of you. Finally, because it is important that the information derived from an interview should be as accurate as possible, the interviewer must be relatively free from prejudice, and the more closely he resembles the candidate in age, sex, interests and social back-

120

ground, the better: remember, you judge other people by inference from your own experience and by analogy with yourself. Although we often seem to be distressingly incompetent at appraising ourselves, when it comes to judging others, the more like us they are the more accurate our assessment is likely to be.

11 Winning and Losing

Despite the widespread acceptance of an anti-success ethos by the young (and the not-so-young) during the late 1960s, most of us are still fascinated by winning and losing. American students continue to vote Harry the man most likely to succeed in the class of '77, while we all dismiss poor old George as a born loser. But what does winning mean? Who are the winners, and how do we recognise them? Social interaction can be seen as a series of competitive encounters, or *life-games*, in which the participants are out to get something from each other, however much they may conceal their intentions beneath a bland, apparently accommodating surface conversation. I don't want to suggest that all social interactions must necessarily be viewed in this way, but it seems legitimate to ask, whenever we see two people in conversation, *why* each of them is talking to the other. It may not always be easy to establish the answer to this question, but when we can do so, it becomes possible to assess, at the end of the conversation, how near each of the participants has come to achieving the goal with which they began it, i.e. what each has got out of it.

Gamesmanship

At the age of four we win by knocking another child over and making him cry, at fourteen, by coming top of the class, and at forty, by convincing a buyer that our product represents better value for money than those of our competitors. In everyday life, to win is to get the better of someone, whether on the battlefield, in the boardroom or the bedroom. Games are played in the most unlikely places. For example, in many of the studies described in this book the experimenters have deliberately deceived their subjects, either by lying about the real purpose of the study or by planting a stooge who is falsely described as another subject. But if the subjects are psychology students they will try to work out the real object of the exercise, which the experimenter wishes to conceal from them until after they have completed the experiment; in this case the experiment is a game in which both experimenter and subject are trying to outwit each other.

Of course, we should miss a lot if we just concentrated on what people say, because the accomplished life-games player can sometimes achieve a quick technical knockout through non-verbal communication before a word has been said. Julius Fast gives some amusing examples of these ploys in his book *Body Language*, and also suggests ways in which we can use non-verbal cues to spot winners. A wife may defer to her husband when they are together in public, but if we notice that whenever she crosses or uncrosses her legs he follows suit soon afterwards, we can guess who has the whip hand in their private marital games.

We most frequently refer to winning and losing in the context of sport or games of skill, but sporting games and life-games often overlap. Sportsmen are supposed to be 'sporting', but a determined competitor won't hesitate to use oneupmanship. The golfer who keeps reassuring the opponent he is beating that it's only a game, knows what he is up to. Games fall into several categories. They may either be *cooperative*, when the players are allowed to communicate and make mutually beneficial arrangements before the game begins, or *non-cooperative*, when they are not. Another important distinction is between *zero-sum* and *non-zero sum* games: in the former, one player's gains are the other's losses, as in poker and most popular gambling games. But in non-zero sum games, what one player wins is not necessarily what the other loses, which is the case in most real-life 'games'. For example, when the boss chats to a junior employee at the office party, the latter gains kudos from the encounter. But the employer hasn't been wasting his time: he has gained a devoted slave to whom in future he can entrust tedious chores. Both begin the conversation with certain objectives and hope to gain different ends. If all goes well, both may emerge as winners. But if something goes wrong – the boss calls John Fred, or John is paralytically drunk – then both may lose.

123

The best-known laboratory game, The Prisoner's Dilemma, is based on an old story about two suspected criminals who are arrested and placed in separate cells. The police are convinced of their guilt, but lack the evidence to convict them of a serious charge. So they tell each prisoner that if he confesses and implicates his colleague, he will get off with a token sentence, but that if he refuses to confess, they will make sure that he is convicted on a trumped-up charge carrying a sentence which falls between the token sentence and the much longer term of conviction for the original offence. Both prisoners face the following dilemma. If neither confesses, both will get middling sentences on the trumped-up charge. But each prisoner runs the risk that the other will confess, in which case he will be convicted of the major crime and receive a very long sentence while his partner gets off with a token sentence. On the other hand, if both prisoners confess, they stand to receive relatively more severe sentences. The best strategy *for both prisoners* is for neither to confess, but since the police make sure that they cannot communicate with each other, they are prevented from coming to an agreement – even supposing that they would trust each other's word if they were allowed to meet!

The dilemma is re-created in the laboratory by separating two subjects and requiring them to make one of two choices, corresponding to the decision not to confess (Choice X) or to confess (Choice Y), in each of a series of games. Instead of prison sentences, the subjects gain or lose sums of money according to the outcome of each game. We may call Choice X a *cooperative* choice, and Y a *competitive* choice, and the figure opposite shows a typical example of the game. If both players choose X, both get a moderate reward; if both choose Y, both forfeit a small amount of money. But if either player chooses Y when the other chooses X, then he can get a very large reward while the other player forfeits an equally large sum. Researchers have found games like The Prisoner's Dilemma which explore cooperation and competitiveness to be an extremely useful way of separating winners from losers. They also reveal that people are far from rational in their view of what constitutes a victory: for example, if you vary the returns, it soon becomes clear that most people are more con-

The Prisoner's Dilemma

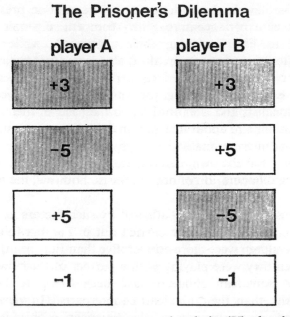

The shaded boxes represent a cooperative choice (X), the plain boxes a competitive one (Y).

cerned with doing better than their opponents than with the actual amount that they themselves receive, which may be a reflection of real-life attitudes towards wages and salaries!

Over a series of games the two players come to cooperate, but what happens in the early stages may vary according to the personality of each participant. People with a strong need for *affiliation* (people, that is, who like to be liked) are very co-operative when not much is at stake, but they become suspicious and highly competitive when there is more to play for. Generally, people dominated by the need to *achieve* and succeed in life are the most trusting and trustworthy in laboratory games, but those whose dominant need is for *power* are found to be consistently uncooperative and exploitative. Touchingly, the latter are most optimistic about receiving cooperation from others.

If we divide people up into competitors and cooperators on the basis of their behaviour in laboratory games, we find that competitors assume that other people will also be competitive, while cooperators are less likely to expect that others will behave as they do. In both cases, the assumption presumably reflects their experience in real life – competitive people tend to provoke us into matching their aggression, while suckers aren't often given an even break. It also seems that behaviour in laboratory games is related to a person's attitudes towards broader issues. One investigator who divided his subjects into internationalists and isolationists, on the basis of their answers to a questionnaire about international relations, war and so on, found that internationalists, though not significantly more co-operative in their own behaviour, were more persistent in seeking the cooperation of others; for isolationists, the opposite applied.

Patterns of play are also affected by such factors as nationality, age and sex. A study carried out in Zambia found that African children were more cooperative than European, though only when they were playing with a partner of their own race; similarly, American children have been found to be more competitive than their Mexican counterparts. (In view of the celebrated competitiveness of the American people, it is surprising to note that the United States is not involved in serious international competition in any major sport.)

Differences observed between the sexes in laboratory games may be influenced by stereotypes imposed on them in childhood. But sex differences in The Prisoner's Dilemma are not what you might expect. A British investigator has found that women playing against other women tend to be *more* competitive than men playing against men; both sexes were less competitive when playing against a member of the opposite sex. The most interesting finding of this study was that people tended to assume that their unknown opponents were of the opposite sex if they behaved in a cooperative manner. In other words, both men and women seemed to expect a greater degree of co-operation from the opposite sex than from their own, in a competitive situation. If further investigation reveals this to be so, it may have important implications for the selection of teams to work together in industry and elsewhere.

What makes a winner tick?

It is difficult to answer this question when we don't yet have an

126

accepted way of establishing what makes *anyone* tick. Probably the most widely used method of assessing human motivation is the projective test, in which you are shown pictures and asked to write down what you think is going on in them, or else just asked to complete a half-finished story. What you write is then analysed for themes which are held to reveal your underlying motivation – for example, the need for power and the need to achieve success or to avoid failure. If you made the main character in your story take decisive action which affected someone else, you would be judged to have a strong need for power. The exercise of power involves getting another person to do something they would not have done without your intervention, but the paradox is that people who have a strong need for power are found to be markedly poor at personal relations, and thus tend to thwart their own ambitions. At a domestic level, studies have shown that the need for power in men is accompanied by a reduced ability either to gain satisfaction from a sexual relationship, or to sustain it for any length of time; interestingly, power-seeking women have not been found to have this problem. The need for power is seen as a neurotic symptom by many psychoanalysts, reflecting either a lack of affection in childhood (Eric Fromm's suggestion) or a feeling of inadequacy (Alfred Adler's); and, after the revelations about life in the White House in the Nixon era, psychologists have been eager to resurrect Harold Lasswell's description of the pursuit of political power as the attempt of a psychologically flawed individual to compensate for his inadequacy.

The balance between people's need to achieve and their fear of failure enables us to predict how they will perform at a competitive task, and it also seems to determine what goals they will set themselves. People whose need to achieve is greater than their fear of failure tend to have goals which are ambitious but within their reach; on the other hand, those who are dominated by the fear of failure set themselves goals which are either so difficult that no one will be able to blame them for not achieving them, or so modest that they can hardly fail. We all know people who somehow never get round to applying for the job their talents would obviously justify or to finishing the book which could make their reputation. We call them perfectionists,

127

because they can't accept that *their* best might not be *the* best. Individuals with an overwhelming fear of failure are probably the nearest we shall come to identifying losers, but since there is no evidence that either the need to achieve or the fear of failure are inherited tendencies, it is inaccurate to speak of a born loser. There are however significant differences in achievement motivation between nations, cultures and even religious groups: it is for example highest in countries with an average temperature of between 40 and 60°F, and higher in predominantly Protestant countries than in Catholic ones. According to David McClelland, a leading researcher in this area, a person's need to achieve can be increased by an intensive training course. Though it has more to do with making money than with making friends and influencing people, the need to achieve is probably the personality factor most closely involved with winning, so anyone interested in becoming a winner should consult McClelland's book, *Motivating Economic Achievement.*

It is sometimes said that women have less need to achieve than men, but there is little evidence for this. In childhood, girls are not dominated by boys – the two sexes tend to play apart – and girls on the whole do better at school, at least up to early adolescence. In adulthood, some studies have found that women on average actually have a *greater* need to achieve than men in neutral circumstances, but that the introduction of stress into the situation tends to boost men's need to achieve while leaving women unaffected. (This finding will come as no surprise to university teachers, who are regularly disappointed by the examination performance of women students who have produced excellent work throughout the course, and astonished by the capacity of men who have devoted their university career to more pleasurable pursuits, to produce the goods when it really matters.) But these studies are fairly old, and at a time when sex roles are very much in the melting pot they may not be a reliable predictor of how men and women will behave in the future. The picture is further confused by the fact that women still tend to be more affected by a different emotion, the *fear of success.* When subjects are asked to complete a story which begins with a member of their own sex enjoying a great success, it is found that women are far more inclined than men to suggest that dreadful things will happen to the protagonist. For example, asked to complete a story which begins with Mary having just heard that she has finished top of her class at medical school, a surprisingly large number of women – themselves students – describe Mary as ugly and unloved, and even quite often have her committing suicide!

Traditionally, people's sex (which is dictated by their chromosomes) has been a very important factor in determining success in life. Some psychologists argue that male supremacy can be justified by the biological differences between men and women. They point out that the aggressiveness of an individual is partly determined by how much testosterone there is circulating in his blood stream, and that testosterone is a male sex hormone. This argument might have had some force in the past, when physical prowess and fighting ability were important aspects of leadership, but studies show that aggression now ranks very low in the list of attributes of a successful leader. The ability to handle people is much more important, and women are at least men's equal in this respect. Biology does not justify the traditional imbalance of power between the sexes; in fact, the pattern of biological and psychological differences between men and women is such that women are if anything better equipped to become winners in the modern world.

Another characteristic which may be associated with winning is Machiavellianism, the knack of manipulating people. This is measured in the laboratory by asking people whether they agree with a number of statements about human nature and life-games tactics, culled from the text of the classic sixteenth-century manual of life-gamesmanship, Niccolo Machiavelli's *The Prince*. Examples of these statements are:

The best way to handle people is to tell them what they want to hear.
Anyone who completely trusts anyone else is asking for trouble.
Never tell anyone the real reason you did something unless it is useful to do so.

On the basis of their reactions to twenty such statements, we can divide people into Machiavellians and non-Machiavellians. Having done so, we find that Machiavellians tend to win laboratory games, especially those which are most lifelike. For example, in one experiment, groups of three subjects (a Machiavellian, a non-Machiavellian, and someone with an intermediate score) were seated round a table with money on it. They were told that any two of them (but not all three) could take the money, provided that they all agreed on how it was to be shared. In every triad studied, the Machiavellian was in the winning pair. In real life, the association between Machiavellianism and success is more complicated. A recent American study of social mobility found that Machiavellians who are also highly intelligent tend to prosper, but that those with a low I.Q. are notably unsuccessful. It seems that an intelligent Machiavellian is able to identify the situations in which his deceitful tactics are likely to succeed, while the stupid Machiavellian employs his wiles counter-productively, merely making his 'victims' determined that he won't get the better of them.

Among university teachers, Machiavellianism is found *not* to be related to academic achievement, but the prospect is somewhat brighter for Machiavellian students. According to another American study, good grades in college are associated with high Machiavellianism – but only for men. For women, good marks were found to have as much to do with physical attractiveness as intellectual ability. So although we may all agree about what's involved in winning, there may be more than one path to victory.

You can't win 'em all!
However much you may polish up your Machiavellian skills or work on your need to achieve, you will never be a winner all the time. So how do we interpret our defeats and victories, and what are the consequences of winning and losing? Where the first question is concerned, laboratory studies tend to confirm popular belief: when people succeed at some task, they attribute it to their own efforts, and when they fail, they blame factors beyond their control ('I'm just not good at this sort of thing'). This reaction to success is probably encouraged by teachers, who on the whole praise children for effort rather than

natural ability, while the reaction to failure is a sensible way of protecting one's self-esteem. Recently it has been confirmed that people apply the same standards in explaining the success or failure of others with whom they identify: when supporters of two Australian football teams were interviewed after a game, a significant proportion of the losing team's supporters attributed the result of the match to pure luck rather than any difference in effort or ability, even though their team had actually been trounced!

But what are the consequences of winning? Does nothing succeed like success, or is failure a spur? These contradictory sayings were put to the test in an experiment in which people had to carry out a variety of tasks in the laboratory, on two occasions. After the first, they were either told that their performance had been good, bad or average, or else no comment was made. Compared with those who had received no comment, subjects who were told that they had done badly did significantly better on the second occasion, whereas those who were told that they had done well did less well subsequently. So, where individuals were concerned, failure did seem to act as a spur. However, when the subjects – groups of American and Dutch adults – were told that they were part of a team who were in competition with another group, a good result at 'half-time' *improved* their subsequent performance. So although individuals may not be encouraged by a good result, teams perhaps are.

Psychology and sport

As the financial incentives and commitments in professional sport have rocketed and winning has become an economic imperative as much as a matter of self-esteem, professional sportsmen have been forced to abandon their scepticism about the advice of scientists and other experts who have never kicked a football in their lives. Increasingly, professional athletes have become willing to act as guinea-pigs, in the hope that research will contribute to the magic formula for success. One of the products of their cooperation is the infant science of sports psychology.

Attempts to pin-point a typical 'athlete's personality profile' have generally failed. There have been straws in the wind –

according to some researchers, there may for example be a 'footballer type', who is emotionally stable, extraverted, tough-minded, radical, of good general ability and ruthless efficiency, and there is also evidence that athletes (particularly those involved in contact sports) possess an unusually high tolerance of pain – but most researchers seem to agree that we cannot at present reliably distinguish sportsmen (let alone *successful* sportsmen) from the general population by using any existing personality test. This may be because successful sportsmen really are no different from the rest of us except in their physical prowess, or it may simply reflect the crudity of personality testing. Perhaps success at sport demands an intricate mixture of attributes which a general test of personality is too clumsy to measure.

But if we know little about what attributes are necessary for an individual to succeed at sport, we do know something about what distinguishes a successful from an unsuccessful team. So far as soccer is concerned, research has revealed that players are more likely – especially when under pressure – to pass the ball to colleagues whom they like, so it is not surprising to find that successful teams get on better with each other than those which are less successful. It is also helpful to have an accepted *playmaker*, to whom a majority of the team are happy to pass, and who will initiate many of their moves. Solitary players may adversely affect the team's efficiency, though soccer forwards are found to be fairly egocentric individuals. At soccer, unsuccessful teams tend to commit more fouls, though when a low-ranking team plays a more successful one, it is the latter who commit the greater number of infringements, a finding which also holds for ice hockey. The 'winners' may feel that their higher status allows them to get away with more, or they may just be less worried by the prospect of conceding a penalty. There is, incidentally, evidence that soccer teams commit more fouls when they are playing away from home (perhaps because they are less likely to be winning, as we saw in Chapter 2), and that high-scoring games are less marred by fouls than goalless ones.

As to motivating players, psychological research suggests that pre-match pep talks are as likely to psych players out as to psych them up. They are already physiologically aroused before a match, and further attempts to whip them up have no effect on good players, and may actually make less accomplished players over-nervous. Especially before a big game it is more useful to concentrate on calming them down, perhaps by encouraging them to use the relaxation techniques described in Chapter 4, as an over-aroused or anxious player is more likely to make errors when put under pressure during the match. The likelihood of this happening can be reduced by the technique of mental rehearsal, in which players while training are told to imagine various crises which may occur during an actual game. They can also be taught to cope with moments of crisis by conjuring up a memory of playing particularly well in a previous match, thus avoiding panic. A player who is out of form can sometimes be helped by being psyched-up. *Assertion training*, in which he is encouraged to behave aggressively (for example by thumping a punch-bag) while thinking about something or someone who annoys him intensely, can benefit his match play, because if he finds himself losing heart during a game, he can imagine the hate-object and regain his will to win.

This brings us to the vexed question of the connection between sport and aggression. At the end of his book *On Aggression*, Konrad Lorenz suggests that one way to deal with what he considers to be our natural aggressive tendencies is to hold more international sporting competitions, on the grounds that watching aggressive games makes us less aggressive, through *catharsis* (purification of the emotions by vicarious experience). Being an avid sports fan I find this an appealing proposition, though hard to reconcile with my experience of the effect which a football match has on my own mood or that of the spectators around me, who no doubt in other circumstances share my mild disposition. Empirical studies confirm that people are *more* aggressive after watching a football match than before it, especially when they identify with either of the teams, although they are unaffected by watching a non-aggressive sport such as gymnastics. Hooliganism at soccer matches has become an international problem, and if you have ever experienced it at first-hand I doubt if you will be convinced by those experts who claim that football crowds display only ritual aggression, and do little actual damage so long as they are allowed to occupy their favourite part of the stadium and to chant their slogans. The causes of football hooliganism remain unclear, but it is a phenomenon which makes Lorenz's solution to the world's problems look a non-starter.

12 Pretending

Man is a make-believe animal: he is never so truly himself as when he is acting a part   W. Hazlitt

You probably feel that there is something rather shameful about the habit of pretending, and it is quite true that it's usually embarrassing for an adult to be exposed as a pretender. The husband who finishes telling an embellished version of a story at a party is put out to discover that his wife has been within earshot, and may feel he has grounds for divorce as she smiles sweetly and murmurs 'Well, it wasn't quite like that, was it, darling?' Similarly, no one likes being found 'conducting' a gramophone record by another person entering the room unexpectedly. Because pretending is often associated with either wickedness or childishness, it isn't something we care to be caught doing. I believe these feelings are misguided, because they stem from an incomplete review of the circumstances in which we pretend. There is actually good reason to suppose that if we were not able to pretend we should find our everyday dealings with other people much more difficult. What is more, make-believe can function as an effective defence mechanism to ward off anxiety, and it can also be a potent medium for changing other people's views.

The Young Pretender
Although adults find it useful to pretend, it is in childhood that we see most clearly the value of make-believe. A study of evolution shows that as we move up through the primates from Old World monkeys through the great apes to man, play seems to become increasingly important in the development of the immature infant. Monkeys and apes have a distinctive way of indicating that what they are doing is playful rather than for

135

real: there is a particular kind of open-mouthed gesture, a slack but exaggerated gait, and a marked 'galumphing' movement, and if one young monkey fails to recognise this signal when it is made by another who wants a play fight with him, then a real fight will take place. But once the signal is recognised, they perform a clownish ballet of mock fighting.

It may seem unnecessary to ask *why* children play, since it is so clear that they (like young apes or young dolphins) find it an intrinsically enjoyable activity. But there is no doubt that play makes a serious contribution to the child's intellectual and social development. Young chimps learn the complex art of termiting by watching their mothers at work, and then trying out in play the various skills which can later be put together when they come to forage for themselves. Similarly, children between the ages of three and five attempting a task which involves clamping two sticks together in order to fish out of a latched box a prize they can't otherwise reach, do better if they have previously been allowed to play with the materials. The crucial point about play is that failure doesn't matter, because the child is 'only' playing; he can therefore use it to practise skills he isn't yet very good at, without being upset when things go wrong. The emphasis which modern educational practice places on play is not just a progressive whim: children of four who show little interest in playing with a new toy are found to be markedly lacking in originality four years later, when they are given a creativity test.

In play, children learn to appreciate the function of symbols and rules – two crossed sticks mean an aeroplane – and they spend as much time making up and discussing the rules as actually playing the game. The outraged reaction of children when one of them refuses to die at cowboys and indians ('I'm not playing if you're not dead!') speaks for itself. It has been suggested that this fascination with rules and the constraints they impose anticipates (and aids in) the tussles which children will have later with other rules such as those of grammar and logic.

Consider the following exchanges between two American four-year-olds:

First child	Second child
Bye Mommy.	
	Bye Mommy.
Bye Mommy.	
	Bye Daddy.
You're a nut.	
	No I'm not.

The children had agreed to the rule that the second child should repeat whatever the first said, but he infringed it, perhaps to see what would happen.

Throughout childhood play and pretence are exploited as children make dry runs before tackling problems in real life. This has the valuable function of helping them to distinguish between fantasy and reality: children playing peek-a-boo with their mothers soon stop exhibiting the sort of distress they may show when she *really* leaves the scene. Adults should be happy to play along with children's pretence, recognising that the distinction between reality and fantasy is an important lesson that has to be learned: being uncertain about it can lead to delusions in adult life, which are often taken to be a symptom of psychopathology. The following exchange, from the same source as that quoted above, shows that four-year-olds are in little doubt about what it is to pretend. The first child sits on a three-legged stool:

First child	Second child
I've got to go to the potty.	
	(Turning to him) Really?
(Grinning) No, pretend.	

We can see, then, that play and pretence are valuable aids to intellectual and linguistic development. Just as important is the role which make-believe plays in social development, as is illustrated in an observation made by the Swiss developmental psychologist, Jean Piaget. The day after a visitor to Piaget's house had become angry, Piaget's infant son threw an unprovoked tantrum in which he clearly mimicked some of the visitor's furious gestures. According to Piaget, this *deferred*

137

imitation plays a vital part in both intellectual and social development, because it enables a child to try out new roles and experiences, to see how it feels to be in someone else's shoes – hence part of the attraction of games like doctors and nurses, mummies and daddies, and so on. The Russian psychologist Vygotsky even describes two sisters playing the role of sisters! They held hands, dressed alike, made a great point of calling things 'ours', and generally acted out the relationship which they actually enjoyed in real life.

Children are often joined by others in their make-believe (one may be the bus-conductor, the others passengers) and it seems that *sociodramatic play* is a necessary stage in children's development. There are individual differences in its incidence – children may be classified as high or low on fantasy – but it is not just a product of Western urban society. The children of bushmen in Botswana, for example, who still lead a nomadic hunter–gatherer life in the Kalahari desert, show a great deal of make-believe in their play based on the subsistence activities of their parents. In industrialised societies 'disadvantaged' children may show less fantasy play, but it is well established that play-tutors can increase the time a child spends playing 'let's pretend', and this sort of training is a feature of many compensatory education programmes. Children can use fantasy play to act out anxieties caused by the demands of their parents, their own aggressive feelings, and so on. This applies particularly to disturbed children; it does not explain the kinds of fantasy play seen in most children, most of the time.

Recent observation of two playgroups in Sheffield suggests that different sorts of fantasy play may have different functions in development. Much of it – playing at shops or giving tea-parties, for example – is fairly sedentary, and involves a lot of object manipulation. But games like monsters or cowboys and Indians are more boisterous, involving rapid changes of role by the participants (spare a thought for the poor researcher who must take note of every occasion when the Dalek turns into Dr Who!). It seems likely that the first sort of fantasy play is more important for language skills and creativity, while the second helps to develop social skills. Although they may encourage the former, teachers tend to intervene to stop rough-and-tumble games. But they are probably wrong to do so, because both types of fantasy play help children to develop into intellectually and socially competent adults.

The Old Pretender

In at least one respect, pretending continues to be a useful and important habit in adulthood. Social psychologists have been struck by the power of what they call the *dramaturgical* model of social behaviour: this follows Shakespeare in regarding the world as a stage, on which we act out roles determined by the situations in which we find ourselves, and proposes that in order to understand why people behave as they do, we must study the demands made by different roles and discover the rules which govern different social situations.

At various stages of life we all have to adopt new positions and responsibilities, and as we feel our way in them we often use the childhood technique of consciously acting out each new role. The student freshman grows a beard, has profound intellectual discussions late into the night, and works in the post office at Christmas (if he's lucky), because he knows that this is how students carry on. Similarly, when your wife is about to have a baby, you turn up at the hospital drunk and pace about chain-smoking, because this is how expectant fathers behave: you've seen them doing it on television. By 'pretending' to be a student or a father you ease yourself into a new role, and make it easy for the rest of the world to see what you have become. Later, when you have gained confidence in your new persona, you may become less self-conscious and more prepared to allow individual idiosyncrasies to creep into your performance.

To pretend is to adopt a role, while being aware of a discrepancy between it and your 'real' self. Once you stop being aware of any distinction and accept the role, you are no longer pretending. In many of our roles, however, there is a continuing ambiguity, with long periods of unquestioning acceptance being punctuated by moments when we *distance* ourselves, standing outside the role and debating our suitability for it. Women, for example, may play at being devoted wives and mothers for years, and then quite suddenly wonder whether this is what they were meant for – if they decide that the

139

costume no longer fits, they may cast it aside and strike out in a completely different role. Playing a role may alter the essential identity of the performer, but the fact that clashes occur between the 'real' and assumed self strengthens the appeal of the dramaturgical approach to social behaviour, and it also confirms the importance of the habit of pretending in our everyday life. How could it be otherwise, when at any given time we all have so many roles in our repertoire? Sitting here in my study, I am the Great Writer. Exhausted by this demanding part, I may wander out into the garden, and before I reach the bottom of the steps I have become the Appreciative Naturelover. Returning to the house, I may have a brief tilt at the Cheese Connoisseur and even – for a few guilty moments – the Pianist Whose Skill Fails to Match his Enthusiasm, before eventually returning to the typewriter. Now these are all roles which I have been playing for some years (admittedly, to rather a small audience), but in all of them you could detect bits of stage-business originally borrowed from other actors I had seen performing them.

The power of roles and the extent of our ability to play-act has been made strikingly clear in a recent experiment in which student volunteers were randomly assigned to two groups and asked to play the part of either prisoners or warders in a simulated prison setting. The researchers intended to keep the experiment going for two weeks, but the performances were so convincing that they had to abandon it after only six days. Afterwards, one shaken 'guard' said: 'I was surprised at myself. I made the prisoners call each other names and clean the toilets out with their bare hands. I practically thought of them as cattle and I kept thinking I have to watch out for them in case they try something'. He was no longer pretending. Roles imposed by institutions like the prison service or the armed forces may be a special case, because they prescribe rights and powers for the actors who perform them. Few roles are as formalised as this – most have a degree of ambiguity which is resolved by agreement with other people who are acting parts around us – but we are all familiar with people who get carried away by their own eloquence in parts such as the heavy father or the jealous husband.

Sometimes we openly admit to pretending, when it is a matter of convenience or convention. When a politician announces that the Cabinet is in unanimous agreement about some controversial course of action, we admire his ability to keep a straight face and recognise that he is making obeisance to the myth of collective decision-making. Similar forms of pretence are binding upon other professional groups: doctors, for example, never question the opinions of their colleagues in front of patients, though they may of course do so in private.

Fiction and drama as therapy
The make-believe world of the play and the novel is another area where pretending is openly acknowledged and accepted, though it is only recently that reading novels has ceased to be regarded as a rather shameful pursuit (the heroines of nineteenth-century novels are for ever being forced to hide the fiction they are reading underneath improving tracts). Drama and fiction are adult versions of 'let's pretend': the author invites us to share a plausible experience and to accept his evaluation of the events described. If we go along with him, he can change our attitudes about the real world. Psychoanalysts have suggested that drama has a deeper significance and a grander function: they regard it as the externalisation of inner psychic dramas (*Oedipus Rex* is the most obvious example), and suggest that the rituals we watch being enacted may change not only our attitudes but the very organisation of our psyches. There is a long tradition which regards drama as cathartic, and part of the attraction of reading fiction stems from the fact that it offers both a respite from the grim reality of everyday living, and the chance either to wallow in someone else's misfortunes or to escape briefly into a utopian world.

In primitive societies, both drama and religion get mixed up with therapy: the ceremonial dramas of the Navaho Indians, for example, are used to cure patients with psychological as well as physical ailments. In our own society the dramaturgical approach has influenced therapists concerned with a variety of psychopathological disorders. In some hospitals, schizophrenics are now encouraged as part of their treatment to act out specified social roles, after which they watch their performance on film and discuss with the therapist ways of improving their social skills. Very recently, at a maximum-security prison hospital in Britain, similar therapy has been introduced for the treatment of sexual offenders, in the belief that they have been driven to seek illicit sexual gratification through their social inadequacy, which prevents them forming relationships which might provide a socially acceptable outlet for their sexual urges.

Unmasking the deceiver

Although it is clear that pretending performs a number of useful functions, we can't ignore its potential as a force for malicious deception. Let us consider three examples, taken from diverse contexts. First, psychologists often want to assess someone's personality, and we know that personality tests are subject to faking when people are asked to answer questions about themselves. In the laboratory this rarely turns out to be a problem, but when tests are given in an applied setting, for example as part of a job selection procedure or in conjunction with a psychiatric interview, people may often try to present themselves in a deceptively favourable light. Fortunately they can usually be spotted, because good personality tests have a built-in lie detector in the form of questions which refer to almost universal faults and very rare virtues: to the extent that the person being assessed denies the former and lays claim to the latter, we can decide whether or not they are trying to pull the wool over our eyes.

Turning once again to the soccer field, the centre-forward who collapses in his opponents' penalty areas as if struck by lightning isn't concerned with the state of his psyche, or anxious to achieve a deeper understanding of the world's problems. Nor does he need any practice in the role of brutally assaulted footballer. He is simply behaving like a good Machiavellian, seeking to manipulate another person – the referee – in order to achieve his goal (in more than one sense).

Finally, in real-life games we seem to accept that people will try to deceive us, and may even not disapprove of them doing so. In an experiment on non-verbal communication, subjects were instructed to ingratiate themselves with a stranger in

142

order to get him to do them a favour. Questioned after the experiment, the strangers (who were also subjects in the experiment) said they had recognised the attempt at ingratiation for what it was, but they regarded the subjects' smiling and gazing as a legitimate tactic. (For the benefit of Machiavellian readers hungry for tips, gazing into someone's eyes may be a more effective way of ingratiating yourself with him than smiling, since the latter is more often perceived as an attempt to influence – but remember the taboo on staring.)

Flattery, trickery and lying all involve pretending, and they, of course, are largely to blame for its bad reputation, which I referred to at the beginning of the chapter. Fortunately there are ways of telling when someone is trying to deceive us – vividly expressed in this quotation from Freud's *Collected Papers* (1905): 'He that has eyes to see and ears to hear may convince himself that no mortal can keep a secret. If his lips are silent, he chatters with his fingertips; betrayal oozes out of him at every pore.' The concept of *leakage* refers to the fact that our bodies will reveal to the experienced observer that we are not speaking the truth. Accomplished liars are notoriously adept at looking straight into your eyes as they pull the wool over them, so there is no point in applying that particular test. Instead, if you suspect that someone is trying to create a false impression, steal a glance at his feet. Because they aren't normally looked at during a conversation, he will probably forget to control them, so they will give him away. After all, why else do you think we describe someone as a shifty individual?

13 Insulting

The insult

I must warn you that you may find parts of this chapter too difficult to understand. Wait! The sentence you have just read is quite untrue, but you didn't know that as you read it, so that can't explain why it probably irritated you. What happened was that I deliberately insulted you. The fact that you are reading this book means that you are claiming to be the sort of person who will understand it; my 'warning' challenged your claim, and that is what made it insulting. We might define an insult as the denial by one person of the identity which is claimed by another. Sometimes this claim is explicit: at the scene of an accident, someone may step forward and say, 'Perhaps I can help, I'm a doctor'. If he gives the wrong advice, this may elicit the scornful comment, 'Some doctor!' More often, the role in which we have cast ourselves – the *identity* we are claiming – has to be inferred from unspoken cues. When my opponent at tennis calls 'out' a service which was clearly 'in', I may mutter, 'Call yourself a sportsman!' He hasn't actually made this claim in so many words, but it is implicit in his presence on the tennis court, and I can insult him by challenging it. It is essential for social ease that the protagonists should respect the *face* of all involved – the image which a person chooses to present in a particular situation. This is most important when two people are talking directly to each other, but it also applies to less direct communication – which is why it is possible for me, the writer, to insult you, the reader.

If you want to insult someone, you must threaten his 'face' deliberately; without malicious intent, you are guilty of nothing worse than a *faux pas*. Some people are renowned for dropping bricks, but they are considered socially naive or inept rather than insulting: their remarks elicit laughter (admittedly rather strained) rather than anger. The accomplished insulter intensifies his attack by leaving open as long as he can the possibility that he is not really meaning to be rude, thus forcing his victim to listen to more abuse than he would have done otherwise. Unintentional attacks on face create embarrassment, and the rules which dictate that face must be maintained are binding on all parties: one is obliged to respect one's own role as much as other people's. It may be less embarrassing when a hostess runs down her own cooking than when a guest does so, but the company still becomes uneasy as they silently ask, 'If this woman really can't cook, why has she invited us to eat her food?'

We usually think of insults as verbal attacks, but it is also possible to launch a non-verbal assault on a person's face. This can be done most effectively by prolonged staring. Convention forbids us to stare at strangers; doing so therefore indicates that we think them so unimportant that they might as well not be there. The man who stares at an attractive woman can hardly claim not to have noticed her, but what he considers to be an admiring glance may infuriate her because of what it tells her about his attitude towards the status of women: to be a sex-*object* is of course to be a non-person. Similarly, the irritation you feel when people at a neighbouring table in a restaurant discuss intimate matters at the top of their voices has less to do with the content of their conversation than with the fact that their behaviour implies that you are too insignificant to warrant the normal courtesies which allow strangers to coexist happily in public places.

Your response

What happens when face is lost? Usually, it's possible to avoid or overlook an insult ('I didn't hear that', 'He's only a child'). But if you choose not to overlook it, the next move is conventionally a challenge in which you draw attention to the violation ('What do you mean, I've got the manners of a pig?'). This invites the other person to repair the situation by making a conciliatory response. He may apologise ('I don't know what came over me'), or make compensation ('I'm always throwing my food all over the place'). Alternatively, he can attempt to change the meaning of his remark ('I was only joking' – the classic back-down – or, 'It was meant as a compliment: I can't stand refined people'). Any of these ploys can make good the damage and restore normal relations, so long as you accept the explanation and the aggressor confirms his penitence with a suitable display of gratitude for being forgiven.

But if the aggressor makes none of these responses when he is challenged, and allows the insult to stand or even adds to it ('And your wife's even worse'), then you have had your bluff called: you are now very close to losing face. There are two alternatives open to you: you can either retaliate ('Well, at least I can hold my drink, unlike some people'), or withdraw with a display of indignation. Either course of action is costly, but you can save some face by withdrawing if, in doing so, you manage to cast doubt on the status of your assailant ('I don't have to listen to this from the likes of you'). At this stage in the game, the relative status of the participants is crucially important: if you are being insulted by your boss, you may have no option but to sit there and take it, with no chance of preserving face.

But what happens when the position is reversed, and the person being insulted enjoys the higher status? In a recent experiment, subjects watched different filmed versions of an awkward encounter between a professor and one of his students. Asked for his opinion of the professor's teaching, the student replied 'Man, this course really sucks', and went on to say, in offensive terms, exactly what he thought had been wrong. The subjects, who were themselves students (though they knew neither of the protagonists), watched the professor replying to this attack in one of six different ways, and were then asked whether they would like to be taught by him. Students who had seen the professor respond either with an aggressive counter-attack, or by agreeing almost tearfully with his assailant's allegations, were clearly unimpressed by him. The most effective reply was found to be a polite, point-by-point refutation of the student's tirade. The investigators suggest that this technique worked best because it enabled the professor to defuse the situation by resolving the conflict introduced by the

146

insult, and also showed that he could defend himself and argue logically.

There are more oblique ways of insulting which exploit the mitigating strategies described earlier (a technique which the writers of the magazine *Private Eye* have developed into an art-form). Humour – including exaggeration and caricature – is supposed to rob insults of their force, a convention which satirists exploit to the full. But the laws of libel recognise that jokes are often taken seriously, so satirists tread a dangerous and sometimes expensive path. Fortunately for them, nothing damns a person more completely than the accusation that he can't take a joke.

When is an insult not an insult?
Ideas about what constitutes an insult, and the appropriate response, differ between cultures and classes, and over time. The cultural differences in the use of space discussed in Chapter 1 are a fertile source of unintentional insults. Arabs who require privacy may simply withdraw into themselves while sitting in a crowded room, whereas a Westerner would seek out an empty room. The Arab's habit of staring intensely into the eyes of the person he is talking to may be seen as over-intimate or even challenging by someone unaware of his customs. I said earlier that only deliberate insults are insulting, but of course the person being insulted has to realise that no offence is intended if none is to be taken.

The notion of face is related to the older concept of honour, and the rituals which surround insulting can be related to the sequence of events which once led to a duel. An insult was delivered and acknowledged; the aggressor was given the opportunity to withdraw it; if he refused, honour could only be satisfied by the sword. This response to an insult is not dead ('Step outside and say that again!'), but it has become much less common. Where once we might have seen actual physical violence, we are now likely to find only *ritual violence*, a phenomenon described by the anthropologist Robin Fox, in his account of 'fights' between rural Irishmen. Following some taunt, the insulter and the insulted go through an elaborate ritual of taking off their jackets, rolling up their sleeves, and squaring up to each other. All the while, both are giving a detailed description of the frightful injuries they propose to inflict on the other, and the pair is surrounded by a crowd of imploring womenfolk, friends who struggle to keep them apart, and interested spectators. But despite (or perhaps because of) all this ritual violence, it is rare for the opponents actually to exchange blows. The exaggerated preparations for battle, the taunts and the threats, seem to be sufficient to satisfy honour, and all concerned eventually adjourn – no doubt to celebrate, in the traditional Irish manner, a diplomatic coup which has prevented blood being shed. This is not unique to rural Irishmen; it is widely accepted as the sequel to an insult when neither the insulter nor the insulted has a taste for actual physical violence, and after it, it is quite common for the protagonists to talk of the good fight they have had. Animals, too, prefer not to inflict physical damage on other members of their own species, most arguments being settled at the jackets-off and squaring-up stage, in favour of whichever can assume the most frightening appearance.

As society has become increasingly complex, the conventions have been relaxed to make it easier for us *not* to be insulted. I think the reason for this is that in the past we were required to play many fewer roles. When people 'knew their place' and were familiar with the parts they were playing, it was assumed that they understood the rules of their social encounters, and therefore there was no hesitation in taking offence when these rules were broken. But we now lack this certainty. Accidental rule-breaking has become commonplace as social distinctions have become more ambiguous, so we can no longer afford to be insulted by slights which would have had our ancestors in the park at first light.

One obvious source of confusion has been the change in the balance of power between the sexes, which has left both sexes less certain about how they should behave to each other. A man who opens a car door for a woman might once have expected to be rewarded with a smile; now, he runs the risk that his action will be construed as an aggressive statement about the relative status of the two sexes, no more welcome than the stare of the lecher we discussed earlier. Similarly, increased

148

social mobility has presented problems about the way we address each other, especially in professional life. In Britain, for example, people of equal rank in jobs which were formerly middle-class preserves, such as the administrative grade of the Civil Service, often referred to each other by their surnames. But since the Civil Service began to broaden its recruitment base this practice has proved a fertile source of unintentional insult, because although those who have had a middle-class education may have learned that the use of surnames implies equality, to the rest of the world it is painfully reminiscent of the way the gentry address their labourers, and officers refer to other ranks.

Form of address has always been a sensitive area, and one easy way to insult someone is simply to use a more intimate form of address than the relationship – or the situation – warrants. In colonial days, French officers were taught to exploit this by using the intimate *tu* with their African soldiers. More recently, black Americans involved in civil rights cases refused to allow court-room proceedings to continue until white southerners agreed to adopt the respectful prefix 'Mr' when addressing them. A distinguished visiting politician recently caused unintentional embarrassment in France by referring to a local politician with whom he was appearing on television by his christian name. The two knew each other well in private life, but the visitor had not been told that such a recognition of intimacy is unheard of in the very formal atmosphere of a French TV studio. His blunder is another good advertisement for the Culture Assimilator programmes mentioned earlier in the book.

Finally, to understand what lies at the heart of an insult, consider the results of the following experiment. American student volunteers were assigned to one of two groups and were asked to read descriptions of themselves written by an observer they had never met. Subjects in one group were described in unflattering terms, while the others read descriptions which were favourable but patently untrue. They were then invited to return the compliment by themselves writing descriptions of what they imagined the person who had described them to be like. From the tone of their retaliatory pen-pictures it was clear that they had been more insulted by an inaccurate description than by an unflattering one. Someone who isn't very bright may actually be more insulted by hearing himself described as brilliant (which he knows is untrue) than by a description which acknowledges his limitations. Overt flattery – when detected – is taken as an insult and hence has the opposite effect to that intended.

14 Believing

An atheist is a man who has no invisible means of support
John Buchan

It is indisputable that religious belief is both a powerful determinant of human behaviour and an important aspect of it. So it is hardly surprising that psychologists, confronted by a major influence on their subject matter (human behaviour) which seems to deny the importance of their guiding principle (empiricism), have been eager to investigate religious behaviour, and even less surprising that they have tended to take rather a dim view of religious belief. Freud described religion as a universal neurosis: in response to the uncertainties of life, man tries to comfort himself by setting up a universal father-figure, God. According to Freud the true believer, by accepting the universal neurosis, is spared the task of forming a personal neurosis.

Michael Argyle, in his book *Religious Behaviour*, has listed seven possible psychological roots for religious belief. The first of these is *direct need reduction*: the religious person can ask for divine assistance when he is ill or wants something. One problem with this suggestion is that, in countries like Britain and America, religious belief is actually less prevalent among the poor than among those whose needs might – objectively – seem less urgent. However, a rich man's needs, though different from those of a poor man, may be no less intense. Secondly, religion may *reduce anxiety* – one psychologist has described religion as omnipresent fear paradoxically turned into bedrock security. There is some evidence in favour of this view. Three-quarters of the soldiers who have been in action report that they were helped by prayer, and old people turn increasingly towards religious belief, though they actually go to church less often, presumably because of their declining physical condition.

Old people who believe in God and in an after-life may view death with greater equanimity than those who do not, though not all investigations have supported this finding.

A third suggestion is that religion is the product of *internal conflict*. Studies show that the Protestant faith is particularly effective at first inducing and then relieving guilt, especially in women. When there is a conflict between one's own wishes and the demands of conscience, it may be helpful to 'project' the latter and experience them as coming from an externalised deity. This projected-conscience mechanism is most likely to apply to Roman Catholics. The fourth possibility is Freud's suggestion that God is a *fantasised parent-figure*, created as a response to neurosis. One objection to both this and the previous suggestion is that religious people in general are not found to be particularly neurotic, though we shall see later that a certain type of religiosity is linked with psychopathology.

The next two possible psychological origins of religious belief concern the way we see ourselves and make sense of what goes on around us. Religious belief may help us to form a concept of ourselves and our place in the scheme of things. We are particularly in need of a crutch for our *ego-identity* during the confusion of adolescence. Many fringe religious sects play on this need, and it is striking that these sects flourish on the outskirts of large American cities amongst communities of immigrants who have been uprooted from stable rural environments. People may join one church rather than another for the social status and the reassuring fellowship which membership of it brings, as they might join a particular political party. There is evidence from America that people change their religious denomination as they ascend the social ladder. We may also adopt religious beliefs for the *cognitive clarity and understanding* they can bring. Science is unable to provide answers to questions like 'What is the meaning of life?' or 'Why are we here?' which we are sometimes moved to ask, especially in late adolescence. Religious belief offers answers which can dispel the unease aroused by such questions, and – paradoxically – provides the believer with greater certainty about matters of religion than he feels about beliefs based on empiricism: a classic study carried out in the 1930s showed that people were more certain about whether there are angels in Heaven than whether there are tigers in parts of China! The need for a crutch to help us understand things is best met by a rigid and dogmatic system of religious beliefs (Roman Catholicism, for example), and studies show that anxious people tend to be the most dogmatic in their beliefs.

Finally, it has been proposed that intense religious experiences may have a *biochemical basis*, because of their similarity to psychotic 'cosmic experiences', which can be mimicked by taking hallucinogenic drugs such as LSD. This suggestion was tested in a rather bizarre experiment in which American theological students listened to a recording of a church service in a chapel on Good Friday, after taking the psychedelic drug psilocybin. Asked to rate the intensity of their religious experience afterwards, the experimental group scored more highly than a control group of their fellow students who had been given the non-psychedelic drug nicotine. The 'tripping' theologians scored particularly highly on feelings of unity, transcendence of time and space, and paradoxicality (the self seeming to dissolve, but enough of the individual remaining to be aware of the mystical experience). Many of the ascetic practices which have been used through the ages to intensify religious experience affect the body's chemistry – flagellation, meditation and sleep-deprivation, for example. Almost 40 per cent of adult Americans polled in a recent survey claimed to have had at least one intense 'religio-mystical experience' (those who made the claim were more often Protestant than Jewish, but more often Jewish than Catholic). The connection between intense religious experience and body chemistry is an intriguing one (though not particularly surprising, since it is after all widely accepted that bodily functions are affected by the mind), but I very much doubt whether many religious people hold their beliefs simply or even primarily in order to change the chemistry of their bodies. Religious belief can allay the believer's doubts about his social position, his intellectual capability, and his moral and mental well-being. (Notice that all these objectives can be achieved, perhaps equally well, by adopting a political ideology and joining a political party.)

Who becomes religious and why?

The *development* of religious belief is very similar to that of political thinking. As a child's first conception of the political leader of his country is dominated by his view of his parents, so God is initially regarded as a big daddy in the sky. Until adolescence, the child's thinking is limited by literalism and concretism: abstracts are beyond him. Intellectual doubts are part of the emotional stress marking the onset of adolescence, and by the age of sixteen most people have decided either to accept or reject religion. The beliefs of his parents are the most important factor in determining whether a person comes to accept religion, and most adults resolve the question in the manner satirised by the poet George Crabbe:

> *Habit with him was all the test of truth*
> *It must be right: I've done it from my youth.*

Childhood experience and emotional factors are more influential than intellectual considerations in deciding whether or not a person holds religious beliefs, even for those who might be thought particularly likely to organise their lives on rational principles. Academics are found to be less likely than most to subscribe to traditional religious beliefs, but a recent study has shown that this is because they tend to come from less religious homes rather than because scholarship reduces religiosity. In the same study, the investigators found that physical scientists, whose work might be expected to make them scornful of beliefs which cannot be supported empirically, were actually more religious than their colleagues in the arts and social sciences. One implication of this finding is that atheists and agnostics, who express astonishment that otherwise 'sensible' people can believe in God, are missing the point that religious beliefs may have little to do with the intellect.

Although most people acquire their adult beliefs gradually, a significant minority of religious adults experience a sudden conversion. A study of Australian theological students found that those who had been suddenly converted tended to be emotionally stable extraverts whose parents were not religious. This supports the psychiatrist William Sargant's suggestion that the stable extravert personality is particularly susceptible to

154

brain-washing. Nor is it surprising that people who have experienced a sudden conversion tend to adopt very dogmatic, fundamentalist forms of religion.

Most investigators now accept that religious belief may take two very different forms. *Extrinsic* religion emphasises the material benefits which are on offer (a subject in one study said that he went to church because it was the best place to sell insurance), while *intrinsic* religion is more concerned with the spiritual side – the development of a philosophy which may provide the basis of a better life, and the opportunity for mystical experience. A number of studies have found that religious people are more authoritarian and prejudiced (and *less* compassionate) than non-religious people. However, it is more likely to be the extrinsically religious who justify the gibe that those who love God most love men least, than the sincerely pious, intrinsically religious people – who unfortunately seem to be in the minority. The finding that religious people in America were significantly more likely than non-religious people to say that Martin Luther King had got what he deserved, when a survey was carried out after his assassination, may well be a reflection of the relative strengths of extrinsic and intrinsic forms of religion in that country. Perhaps only extrinsically religious people use religion as a projective device to deal with their anxieties: it has for example been found that the concept of the deity is more sophisticated – and less likely to resemble a person's view of his parents – among those who have had more intense religious experiences. Projective, extrinsic religion may be viewed as a less mature form of religiosity, and it is possible that you can only advance beyond it to a position of intrinsic belief if you have access to sophisticated religious teaching.

You might expect religious people to be different from non-believers in other ways – there might be a distinctive 'religious personality', perhaps marked by a proneness to psychopathology. But in fact, possibly because of the two opposite forms religiosity can take, investigators have had little success in tying religious belief to specific personality factors, nor have they been able to confirm Freud's suggestion that religion and psychopathology are frequent bedfellows. Some have been

155

impressed by the fact that religious preoccupations are common in the early stages of psychotic illness. There is a school of thought which suggests that schizophrenia should not be regarded as a crippling and distressing illness, but rather as an admirable and constructive, essentially religious attempt on the part of the schizophrenic to assimilate some aspect of the ultimate meaning of life. I am unimpressed, to say the least, by this view of schizophrenia, not only because it relies heavily on the reports of patients whose grip on reality may be uncertain, but also because I am doubtful that it has advanced the interests of the schizophrenics themselves. In fact, religious preoccupations were much more common among schizophrenics in the nineteenth century; now they are more likely to see terrestrial machines with wires, electricity and X-rays – even radar or television – as being responsible for their delusions.

But although religious people in general seem similar to those who are not religious, consideration of people holding extreme or esoteric religious beliefs confirms the view that religion is a crutch for psychological inadequacy. If we agree with Marx in regarding religion as the opium of the people, let it be clear that we are referring to the tranquillising rather than the stimulating properties ascribed to that drug. If you have ever spent time on a Sunday morning in discussion with a Jehovah's Witness, you will not need to be told that members of that sect adhere to their beliefs with a disquieting conviction which provides strong grounds for suspecting that they are using its dogma as a crutch to support inner uncertainty. Between 1971 and 1973 there were 7456 admissions to Western Australian mental health hospitals, and fifty of these patients were Jehovah's Witnesses. Given the total population of the catchment area (more than a million) and the total number of Jehovah's Witnesses within it (about 4000), it is clear that the movement is over-represented. More detailed analysis reveals that the incidence of schizophrenia in the sect was three times as high as in the general population, and rates of paranoid schizophrenia were nearly four times as high. These figures might indicate that belonging to the sect increases – for some unknown reason – the likelihood that an otherwise normal person will become schizophrenic, but it seems more plausible to suppose that there is something about the sect which appeals to already disturbed individuals. In other words, the beliefs are being used as a crutch, albeit (the figures suggest) not a totally effective one.

Rather different are the sects based on Eastern religions which have flourished in the United States and Western Europe over the last decade. A New York psychiatrist recently investigated the motivation of fourteen disciples of one Baba, a former insurance salesman who had spent two years in India with the guru Sai Baba. All but one of the followers said they had had an unhappy childhood, and most expressed feelings of sexual or emotional inadequacy. Only four had not previously undergone psychotherapy of some sort, and all reported that joining the sect had given them a feeling of euphoria based on a new sense of acceptance and security, and a relief from guilt and inhibition. They too were clearly using religious belief as a crutch.

Is religion really on the decline?

This question is confused by evidence that the distinction between believers and non-believers is less sharp than you might suppose. Most detailed studies have supported the popular assumption that there is a continuing decline in conventional religious beliefs and practices. For example, a recent survey of British university students found a marked decline in religious belief, the habit of praying and church attendance, in both men and women, between those admitted in 1961 and 1972. Significantly, the proportion of students who had received no religious upbringing had increased fourfold over this period, and the investigators explained their findings by suggesting that the social forces inimical to religion had begun to operate earlier in people's lives, rather than having increased in intensity. In other words, today's students are less likely than their predecessors to have parents and teachers who encourage religious belief, an explanation which supports what I have already said about the early development of religious beliefs.

We have to interpret these findings with caution, however, because a surprisingly large number of people who are considered to be non-believers admit to having religious experiences. The American survey already cited implies that some 46 million Americans may have had some kind of intense religious experience – far more than there are active members of religious groups. Other studies confirm that many people who are not attached to any religious organisation (and are therefore officially classified as non-believers) actually believe in God, admit to religious experiences, and even attend churches. So although the membership of organised religious groups may be on the decline, it is clearly unwise to assume that personal religious beliefs are declining at the same rate.

It is interesting to note that the decline in religiosity has taken place at the same time as a decline in political ideology. A recent analysis of the policies put forward by the major political parties in twelve different countries (including America, Russia and most Western European nations) found that there had been a significant convergence of policies between parties of the right and the left over the last fifty years, with the greater softening of policies taking place on the right. If the acceptance of religious beliefs or political ideology is an indication of psychological weakness – only the inadequate need dogma to support them – this pattern of social change seems to offer grounds for optimism, though we may merely be transferring the weight of our inadequacy to different crutches.

15 Walking

You are walking along a narrow corridor or pavement when you notice someone approaching from the opposite direction. Your paths converge, and at the critical moment you swerve to one side to let him pass. But alas, he guesses wrong, and simultaneously moves the same way. You both halt to avoid a collision, exchange apologetic smiles to show that no harm was intended, but then simultaneously take a step in the opposite direction, and so end up face-to-face once again. Occasionally, further bobbing and weaving in unison ensues, and the situation begins to look like a rehearsed dance routine. Never one to miss a dark innuendo, Freud has described these encounters as improper and provocative pieces of behaviour, in which we are trying to disguise sexual aims behind a mask of clumsiness. Since there is not a shred of evidence to support this interpretation, I prefer to regard them as genuine misunderstandings. But perhaps the most striking feature of such encounters is how rarely they occur, and how efficiently we generally manage to rescue ourselves when they do.

The fact is that we are extremely accomplished at walking – which is just as well, because we spend a large portion of our lives doing it. That we also seem to be aware of its importance as a skill is perhaps the reason why parents attach inordinate significance to the first steps of a baby: with the exception of talking, no other developmental landmark is more eagerly awaited. One reason for this may be that it is an accomplishment which serves so many ends. Not only is walking still the commonest way of getting from A to B, but it has become, over the last half century, an increasingly popular form of recreation: upwards of five million Britons are estimated to walk for pleasure, and the British are by no means unique in this respect. We also walk to pass the time – because it implies a purpose, walking is a useful way to disguise the fact that we have arrived somewhere five minutes early – and for a host of other purposes in social life. To take a trivial example, we may just stamp about in order to annoy the people in the room below.

More importantly, we accept that a person's walk may be a revealing individual characteristic. When asked how they set about building up a new role, many actors say that they develop the walk of a character first, and it is significant that when we are asked to imagine another person's feelings, we speak of putting ourselves in his shoes. Everyday language also makes it clear that we don't regard walking simply as a means of getting from one place to another – we say that someone moves purposefully or dejectedly. And they don't only walk: they stride, shuffle, sneak and slink. Since we use these terms without necessarily seeing the face of the person whose motion we are describing, we must assume that the apparently straight-forward action of changing location by putting one foot in front of the other is rich in information about the mood and the intentions of the walker. This is why walking is such a fertile source of humour: the Ministry of Silly Walks sketch in the TV show *Monty Python's Flying Circus* exploits the fact that because we all know what walking ought to look like, we have no difficulty in recognising a silly walk. Not, of course, that John Cleese was the first comedian to realise this – Charlie Chaplin and Groucho Marx are both instantly recognisable by their distinctive walks.

A neglected art
Since walking is both a regularly occurring and a very useful habit, you might perhaps assume that psychologists would have devoted as much attention to it as they have to other frequent and important pieces of behaviour like sleeping, eating or social interaction. But you would be wrong. Walking is a neglected art, which illustrates a general point that habits are things we do without thinking, and that the less thought we give to per-forming them, the less likely they are to come to mind when we start thinking about our behaviour. However, walking is not the mindless automatic business you might suppose. If you ask someone who is walking along to multiply 17 by 9, he will stop

to do the sum, which shows that walking requires some attention. It is only very recently that psychologists have woken up to its importance, with the result that the psychology of walking is still in its infancy. Equally surprising is the attitude of urban planners towards what remains the commonest form of transport. Our cities are increasingly organised to meet the demands of those who travel by car, despite the fact that the majority of journeys undertaken in cities are by foot. Certainly, measures are taken to 'protect' pedestrians, but they reflect the tacit assumption that walkers must give way to motorists where the interests of the two clash. For example, barriers are constructed at points where pedestrians are most likely to want to cross the road, and subways designed to prolong the walker's life have the same effect on his journey.

Those who suffer most from the planners' priorities are children and old people, who are least likely to have access to automobiles. Since, on other grounds, we might regard these as groups who deserve especially favourable treatment, it seems clear that psychologists are not alone in giving walkers the cold shoulder. In fact, psychologists are beginning to remedy their neglect, and a recent study has cast much-needed light on one of the major anxieties of parents – the fear that their children will be killed or maimed while crossing the road. When an American psychologist asked a large number of children between the ages of five and fourteen to estimate the speed of oncoming vehicles, he found that certain types of car, moving at certain speeds, are especially likely to deceive children. Specifically, noisy vehicles frighten children more than quiet ones, but this has the effect of making children overestimate their speed, and stay on the pavement. So although noisy cars and lorries may be a nuisance in other respects, they seem to be safer from the child's point of view than a quieter vehicle. One unexpected finding was that although older children were better than younger ones at judging speeds up to 40 miles an hour, children below the age of nine or ten were actually more accurate at assessing faster speeds. This may be because younger children tend to judge that all cars are going faster, since, being themselves physically smaller, everything seems faster. British studies have also shown that a majority of child pedestrian accidents occur on the far side of the road, which suggests that children are looking in only one direction before setting off and neglecting traffic on the other side of the road, and that 80 per cent of the children are running when they are struck by a car. So far as the *reasons* for the accidents are concerned, a complete lack of attention is most often the cause for children beneath the age of ten, whereas a partial lack of attention seems to be the dominant factor in the ten to fourteen age group. Taken together, these findings could form the basis of a more effective programme for teaching children how to cross the road in safety.

Walking in cities leads us to one area where scientists have acknowledged that walking is an activity worthy of their attention. The speed at which people walk has been used as an index of the pace of life, to test the widely held belief that urban life is more hectic than small-town life (other rural–urban differences were discussed in Chapter 2). In one study, observers noted the average length of time it took to walk 100 feet after leaving a bank, and found this to be significantly longer in a small town in Iowa than in New York or Washington D.C. Emboldened by this discovery, scientists at the Max Planck Institute in Munich have recently published the results of a cross-cultural investigation of walking speeds measured at fifteen different locations in Europe, Asia and North America. A comparison between the average speeds in cities and towns (with more or less than 200,000 inhabitants respectively) confirms that city dwellers walk almost half as fast again as people who live in towns. It has been suggested that this reflects the difference in population densities: perhaps we are over-stimulated by the crowds which surround us on city pavements, and walk faster to minimise the amount of time we spend in the vicinity of fellow pedestrians. It may also be that, in crowded conditions, the norms which prevent us walking too fast become less important than the unspoken rule which dictates that we must not slow down the speed at which most people are moving.

The pedestrian navigator
Very recently, social psychologists have begun to analyse walking as a skilled performance, or accomplishment, and to

catalogue the non-verbal cues which prevent mayhem breaking out on a crowded pavement. The fundamental problem is navigational: how do we manage to avoid collisions, without the aid of the motorist's horns, indicators and elaborate code of hand-signals? Looking at the oncoming pedestrian traffic, we first have to decide how it is organised: who is walking together and who alone? Convention dictates that the solitary walker must acknowledge the unity of an approaching group by walking round it; to do otherwise is considered rude or even provocative – groups, like individuals, need *personal space* (see Chapter 1). If the group is too big to be circumnavigated, it usually breaks up into smaller units to allow the lone walker to pass without breaking the rules, and it is the failure to do this which causes, for example, office workers in cities which are popular with tourists to become angry with large parties of visitors. People who are walking together can demonstrate the fact in a number of ways: they may be holding hands or talking to each other, but the most reliable sign of togetherness is deliberately maintained proximity. This is most apparent when an obstacle is encountered or a corner turned – by adjusting their pace to re-establish contact with others, pedestrians make it clear that they are walking together, and not merely along the same stretch of pavement at the same speed. This latter – 'accidental' walking together – is actually a source of embarrassment, because it may be construed as spying or as a clumsy attempt at a pick-up. We therefore go out of our way to avoid it, altering our pace or even crossing the road in order to avoid having our behaviour misinterpreted.

The basic objective of someone walking along a crowded thoroughfare is to reach his destination without colliding with other travellers, and the techniques we use to achieve this goal were clearly demonstrated in an observational study of pedestrians on 42nd Street in New York. An experimenter selected pedestrians who were walking in the middle 'traffic lane', where the rule was every man for himself, and approached them on a collision course from a distance of between 25 and 50 feet. He or she wore dark glasses to avoid making eye-contact with the victim, and only took avoiding action at the last moment, on the few occasions when it became apparent that the target pedestrian was not prepared to do so. The details of each encounter were recorded on film shot from a window over-looking the street. Normally, the unwitting subject gave way at a distance of about 7 feet when traffic was light, and about 5 feet when the pavement was more crowded. When the conditions allowed it, pedestrians tended to change course to permit the experimenter to pass, but when the pavement was very crowded they used a routine which the investigators christened *step-and-slide*, in which they angled their bodies, turned their shoulders, and made a small side-step. To be effective, this requires cooperation from the person approaching, and the intensity of the remarks addressed at the experimenters when they failed to provide such cooperation ('Whatsa madda? Ya blind?') confirmed that we confidently expect other people to obey the rules of pedestrianism, and are extremely put out when they do not. Having been forced to change their route by the ruthless experimenters, subjects almost invariably reverted to their original path – an apparently pointless manoeuvre, which wasted time – unless their goal was actually off their original course, in which case they made a bee-line for it.

The same investigators observed that when we are walking in the same direction but *behind* someone else, we try to keep a distance of at least 5 feet between us, and walk slightly to one side of them in order to look over their shoulder; we only walk directly behind someone who is more than 15 feet in front of us. This strategy enables us not only to monitor the route ahead, but also to avoid bumping into the person in front, which is important because, as with motorists, it is conventional that the pedestrian behind always takes the blame for a collision. One consequence of this elaborate ritual is that when large numbers of people are walking along, anyone who alters his course forces those behind him to adjust their route, in order to maintain their head-over-shoulders relationships with the people in front; such mass movements can be seen in films of crowded thoroughfares. A final observation made in this study was that children of less than seven are treated as baggage, both by the parents who drag them along, and by other pedestrians, who buffet them without showing much concern. The question

164

of how children acquire the skills which make them accomplished pedestrians as adults is still waiting to be explored.

Social psychologists at Oxford have also studied the problem of how people manage to avoid collisions on pedestrian crossings. They filmed four hours' activity on one such crossing, and coded the body movements made by individuals at the moment when they passed someone coming the other way. They found that men and women adopt quite different strategies to avoid collisions in these circumstances: men tend to face the person they are passing, while women turn their backs on them, regardless of their own age, and the age and sex of the other person. Since women are also more likely to cross their arms as they pass, the Oxford workers drew the unexceptionable conclusion that they are concerned with protecting their breasts during these encounters.

So far, we have confined ourselves to discussing how we cope with other pedestrians who share crowded pavements with us; but what happens when we have to walk past, or even through, a stationary group of people? A number of investigators have explored this question. In one study, pedestrians were filmed as they walked past a bench in a hallway, either when it was empty, or when various numbers of people were sitting on it. It was found that the more people seated on the bench, the wider the berth it was given by pedestrians, which suggests that the personal space requirements of a group are a product of the individual requirements of each of its members. And when two stooges were placed in a narrow public thoroughfare, people tended to walk round rather than between them (as we might expect from the findings discussed earlier), though only when the two stooges were engaged in conversation. However, when they did walk between them, people tended to dip their heads as if in apology, and often engaged in behaviour which was strongly reminiscent of the displacement activity which animals show when they are uncertain about what to do (for example, they 'groomed' themselves by smoothing down their hair), which may indicate that they were uneasy about what they were doing, and worried about a possible violation of personal space.

There is one situation in which walkers seem to lose their

cool, and behave in an irrational way. Walking alone along a street seems, on the face of it, to be a very private activity. But when a lone walker discovers that he has made a mistake – taken the wrong turn or walked past his destination – he will often react as if everyone were watching him. He will either try to disguise his error by stopping to gaze into a shop window, the contents of which actually are of no interest to him, or else acknowledge it with an ostentatious 'silly-me!' gesture. Either response suggests that the walker feels that he is on display, but this is quite unjustified. Although we are constantly aware of the intentions of fellow pedestrians, this is entirely unconscious: we are alert to them as walking-machines, not as people.

16 Smoking

We are a society addicted to and obsessed with smoking. Nor is this in the least surprising. After all, everyone is interested in money and health, and in Britain the tobacco habit not only contributes to at least fifty thousand premature deaths every year but also provides between five and ten per cent of the government's annual revenue. For a psychologist, there is an additional reason for studying smoking. According to the results of a recent survey carried out in Britain, three out of every four adults polled believed that smoking increases the risk of developing lung cancer, but at the same time almost half of them admitted to being regular smokers. Now it has long been an accepted principle of human motivation that, when we have the choice, we tend to do things which either lead to pleasure or help us to avoid pain (this is called the hedonic principle). Smoking therefore seems to pose a serious problem for the behavioural scientist: how is he to explain a habit indulged in by every other adult, a majority of whom are aware that it may lead to discomfort, pain and even premature death?

There are two let-outs. To the extent that the smoker is a nicotine addict, we may deny that he really *chooses* a behaviour with unpleasant consequences; and because these consequences are long-term, at least during the years in which the habit tends to be formed, they are easy to ignore. There is evidence that smokers who manage to break the habit do so not because they fear the risks but because they are already suffering from one of the illnesses associated with smoking. But unless we can produce evidence that smoking has significantly rewarding short-term effects we may still have to replace the hedonic principle with some less appealing account of human motivation.

The effects of smoking

Such theoretical considerations, as well as the more obvious practical ones, explain the enormous research effort which has been devoted to smoking, as a result of which we now know a lot about why people smoke, who smokes what and when, and why the habit is so difficult to abandon. But what actually happens when you smoke and inhale a cigarette? The effects need to be divided into two classes, twice, because there are physiological and behavioural consequences which may be short-term or long-term. 'Effects' is perhaps too strong a word to apply to some of the subtle associations we shall be discussing. For example, it is not easy to decide on the evidence available whether smoking really leads to lung cancer or whether the sort of person who becomes a smoker is also the sort of person who, for some quite separate reason, perhaps genetic in origin, is also predisposed to contract the disease. A survey of 34,000 British doctors found that between 1953 and 1965 their consumption of cigarettes dropped dramatically. At the same time, deaths from lung cancer among them dropped, although during this period the proportion of lung-cancer deaths among the general population increased. Conclusion? Smoking leads to lung cancer. But wait a minute. In pairs of identical twins where one smokes and the other doesn't, both are equally likely to die from lung cancer. Conclusion? It's all a matter of genes. (It's tempting to say that the only thing which has been proved beyond reasonable doubt is that smoking is one of the leading causes of statistics!) The picture is further confused by making international comparisons. The Japanese smoke almost twice as many cigarettes per person as we do but have only a fifth of our lung-cancer mortality rate. At present, all we can say about the link between smoking and lung cancer is that smoking is neither a sufficient nor a necessary cause of lung cancer, because not all smokers develop lung cancer and not all lung-cancer patients are smokers. On the other hand, smokers are almost ten times as likely to develop the disease as non-smokers. Our inability to say that smoking *causes* lung cancer may simply be a reflection of more general ignorance about what causes lung or any other form of cancer.

The short-term physiological consequences of inhaling

cigarette smoke are relatively unambiguous. There are three active ingredients: nicotine, tar and carbon monoxide. When you inhale, there is an instantaneous tingling 'nicotine scratch' as the smoke stimulates receptors in the mouth and respiratory tract. Nicotine, which is responsible for most of the positive effects, passes from the lungs and mucous membranes in the nose and mouth to the brain via the cardiovascular system. It passes freely through the blood–brain barrier, so that its psychoactive properties rapidly make themselves felt.

Generally speaking, small doses of nicotine – cigarettes contain from 0.1 to 2.0 milligrammes – function as a stimulant. (Other stimulants include caffeine – found in coffee, tea and such fillers as coca-cola – which is less powerful than nicotine, and dexedrine, which is more powerful.) Stimulants alter the electrical activity of the brain to make you more alert and aroused, and it is these changes which are behind most of the beneficial consequences of smoking. Experiments show that nicotine in the dosage obtained by smoking three average-strength cigarettes an hour is a very efficient way of sustaining the performance of tasks which demand vigilance over long periods of time. In a simulated driving situation, for example, smoking has been found to prevent the deterioration usually observed as time goes by. This is a finding of some social significance, especially in conjunction with the recent discovery that nicotine seems to protect smokers from the deleterious effects of alcohol, even in doses significantly higher than that permitted to drivers by current legislation. Surveys suggest that for every 'drunken' driver stopped by the police there may be as many as four thousand motorists on the roads with illegally high blood-alcohol levels. Some of these of course will have drunk so much that not even the most massive dose of stimulants could make them fit to drive, and the fact that they are not stopped is a matter of luck or a reflection of the shortage of policemen. But the smokers among them may be driving at their normal, sober level of efficiency, as the stimulant properties of nicotine ward off the depressant effect which all but the smallest doses of alcohol have on the brain. Since the health risks associated with smoking have been so well publicised, it seems only fair to draw attention to one circumstance in which lighting up a cigarette may actually *improve* rather than detract from your standing as an insurance risk. The experiments on which the drunken driving laws based their calculations of 'safe' blood-alcohol levels were performed on subjects who were not allowed to smoke; if smokers were not such a downtrodden section of the community, they might with some justification lobby for a more liberal criterion of functional drunkenness for themselves!

In the laboratory, nicotine has been shown to reduce the time it takes to perceive and react to stimuli, and also, in animals, to improve memory and learning ability – all of which might be expected on the basis of the drug's effect on one's ability to pay attention and concentrate. More surprisingly, it seems to reduce aggression in rats. No one has yet attempted to extrapolate from this finding to human behaviour, though motorists who smoke may be tempted to derive from it further vindication for their much-abused habit.

Turning to the debit side, nicotine causes the hormone nor-adrenalin to be released into the blood. This pushes up the blood pressure and mobilises fatty acids from the body's fat stores; as a result, there is an increase in both the amount of oxygen the heart requires and the level of cholesterol in the blood. Just as damaging is the injury inflicted on the fine hairs in the windpipe and bronchial tubes by tars in the burning tobacco. These hairs are the basis of an elegant natural cleaning system which encourages us to cough out irritant particles or bacteria we may have inhaled, and for which the smoker's cough and ritual morning hawking is a very poor substitute.

Tar is the element in cigarettes which increases the likelihood of a smoker contracting chronic bronchitis (and maybe lung cancer), but carbon monoxide is responsible for the connection between smoking and coronary heart disease. Adding a filter-tip to a cigarette reduces its tar–nicotine content but increases the amount of carbon monoxide inhaled, because the paper surrounding the filter is relatively non-porous and thus prevents the gas from escaping as smoke is drawn towards the mouth. In Britain between 1956 and 1973 there was a dramatic change in smoking habits, away from plain cigarettes towards those with filters; during this period the number of deaths from lung cancer amongst men under 60 actually declined (despite little change in the number of cigarettes smoked), whereas death from coronary heart disease in this group increased.

Who smokes and why

Why do people smoke? Why is one person a smoker while another is not? Early researchers assumed there must be a single reason for smoking, and therefore looked first for differences between those who smoked and those who did not. The results of this research were disappointing: such differences as there were tended to be small. Generally speaking, smokers were found to be more extravert and restless than non-smokers. They tended to drink more (it is certainly true that the vast majority of hospitalised alcoholics are heavy smokers, and laboratory studies show that smokers automatically increase their cigarette consumption when they are drinking), to get married and divorced more often, to move house and change jobs more often, and to spend more time in hospital.

We might also expect to find physiological differences between smokers and non-smokers. The average smoker spends about two hours a day with a lighted cigarette, and about eight minutes of this time inhaling cigarette smoke. Each puff gives him a shot of about 100 microgrammes of nicotine as directly as if it had been injected (it is this rapidity of absorption – and the consequent immediacy of its effects – which makes addicted smokers so dependent on cigarettes). Since people who smoke more than ten cigarettes a day are maintaining themselves at a fairly permanent, definite drug level, it is not surprising to find neurological differences between smokers and non-smokers. The clearest physiological difference can be seen in EEG records: heavy smokers tend to show a lot of high-frequency activity in the brain and very little alpha rhythm (the brain correlate of relaxation), and indeed find it difficult to produce alpha rhythm by means of techniques like meditation. When smokers are deprived of cigarettes for 24 hours they may show a significant increase in slow-frequency brainwaves, but this is accompanied by a mixture of drowsiness and restlessness as well as a general feeling of ill-being.

Theorists who treat smokers as a single class have also

looked for a single cause for smoking. The most influential of these theories is based on the notion of physiological arousal. We have seen that nicotine makes us more aroused – we probably smoke more when drinking so that we can remain sufficiently alert to appreciate the effects of alcohol. Some people have a lower natural level of arousal than others, so if we assume that there is a best-possible level of brain arousal at which we would all like to operate, much human behaviour can be explained as an attempt to reach this point. H. J. Eysenck has suggested that introverts are naturally highly aroused individuals who require little further stimulation from the outside world, and therefore become cautious loners. Extraverts on the other hand have less spontaneous activity in the brain and so attempt to boost their level of arousal by seeking out excitement and fun. On this analysis, we should certainly expect smokers to be extravert, and there is some evidence that the more extraverted a smoker is, the more cigarettes he smokes a day. But introverts also smoke, so it seems very unlikely that the only reason people smoke is to stimulate themselves, even though we know that smokers generally, but particularly males who smoke heavily, reduce their consumption when they are aroused by other means, for example by a lot going on around them.

The simple theory that smokers light up to increase their arousal level is also unable to explain the link between smoking and anxiety: the more anxious you are, the more likely you are to smoke. Giving up smoking tends to make people more anxious, and less anxious smokers find the habit easier to break. Since anxiety is an emotional state associated with *high* arousal, it looks as though some people light a cigarette when they want to become more aroused and others when they wish to reduce their level of arousal. Some researchers have linked the different reasons for smoking to differences between the sexes, women being more likely to use tobacco as a sedative and men using it as a stimulant, but a recent study found no such difference. Actually, there is some doubt that cigarettes are of use as a sedative. It is more likely that the dramatic effects of nicotine on the body – the smoker's heart-rate is raised by about twelve beats a minute shortly after lighting up, and this effect continues up to twenty minutes after the cigarette has been stubbed out – relieves anxiety by distracting attention from anxiety-provoking events in the outside world.

Detailed examination of the reasons why people smoke suggests that there are six factors involved, each underlying a different sort of smoking. These are: stimulation, indulgence, psychosocial, sensorimotor, addictive, and automatic smoking. They are different types of smoking rather than different types of smoker, but individual smokers have predominant patterns of smoking. If you are a smoker, you may judge how influential each factor is for you by checking how closely your own behaviour matches the stereotypes given in the table below.

Smoking type	Distinguishing characteristics
Stimulation	More likely to light up when working hard or rushed
	Smoke when tired or to feel more alert
	Find smoking helps thought and concentration
	Smoke to cheer yourself up
Indulgence	Smoke mostly when comfortable and relaxed
	Smoke only when time to sit back and enjoy it
	Smoke when having a quiet rest
	Find smoking most enjoyable after meals
Psychosocial	Get on better with people when smoking
	Enjoy offering and accepting cigarettes
	Feel more confident and sophisticated when smoking
	Smoke much more when with others
Sensorimotor	Smoke for the pleasure of having something to put in the mouth
	Find handling a cigarette pleasurable
	Find the business of lighting up enjoyable
	Find pleasure in watching the smoke as it is blown out
Addictive	Find it almost unbearable to run out of cigarettes

Feel a gnawing hunger to smoke if too long between cigarettes
Don't know what to do with hands without a cigarette
Smoke without being aware of it

Automatic   Smoke without remembering lighting up
Light up while previous cigarette still alight
Smoke without being aware of it

Giving up

These categories are not mutually exclusive, and the behaviour of most smokers reflects to varying degrees the influence of more than one factor. Also, the factors fall into two distinct groups in a way which enables us to answer the question, why do people smoke? If you are primarily an indulgence or a psychosocial smoker, your reasons for smoking have little to do with the effects of nicotine. Perhaps you find the ritual comforting, the associations pleasant, or just enjoy doing what others around you do: smokers are more likely than non-smokers to have family and friends who smoke. You are not addicted to the habit and so should be able to give it up without too much distress. If you want to do so, whenever you feel the need to smoke, go and sit by yourself somewhere which is cold, uncomfortable and generally unpleasant. Alternatively, force yourself to smoke three times your normal daily consumption for a few days. Either course of action should change your feelings about the habit and help you to give up – provided that you really want to.

If your smoking fits into the stimulation, addiction and automatic categories you are pharmacologically addicted to nicotine, and your chances of being able to give up are less good. According to the statistics you are most likely to give up if you contract some ailment directly attributable to smoking (a painful cough, breathlessness or a heart complaint); then you should stop smoking abruptly and completely, surround yourself with non-smokers, and give yourself powerful extra incentives not to smoke. Three out of four regular smokers try to abandon the habit; only one succeeds. Mark Twain, whose smoking habits can be deduced from two of his rules for living – never smoke more than one cigar at a time; never smoke when asleep or refrain when awake – described giving up smoking as the easiest thing he ever did. He spoiled the effect by adding that he ought to know, because he had done it a thousand times.

There are more dramatic techniques for giving up smoking. Aversion therapy has been used, in which smokers are given a painful electric shock as they light up a cigarette, but the opportunity for contact and discussion with the therapist and other sufferers during these sessions is actually found to be just as effective without the shocks. Extravagant claims have recently been made for a technique which combines sensory deprivation, propaganda and relaxation. Smokers are left without cigarettes for 24 hours in a darkened sound-proof room. They are then asked at intervals over an intercom to imagine worrying situations in the past in which they have smoked heavily, and encouraged to practise relaxation exercises. It is, however, too early to judge whether this mild form of brainwashing will really prove effective.

Propaganda, whether from advertisers or as part of a public health campaign, does have some effect, at least on attitudes and opinions: a majority of the British public were sceptical about the link between smoking and lung cancer in 1967, but after an intensive propaganda campaign three out of four people now believe in it (rightly or wrongly). But does propaganda affect behaviour? An ironic set of events in the United States suggests that it can. When cigarette advertising was still permitted on American TV, the networks were required to broadcast a certain number of announcements about the health risks of smoking. When the commercials were banned in 1971 the number of compensatory health messages also dropped, and the net result was a significant increase in the number of cigarettes per head smoked over the next twelve months.

For the addicted smoker unable to give up, a change to mild cigarettes is unlikely to be effective. You may just smoke more of them, increasing your exposure to carbon monoxide and the chances of rupturing yourself trying to get enough nicotine into a puff to satisfy your habit. Since 1974 mild, low-tar (low-

175

nicotine) cigarettes have raised their share of the market in Britain from 5 to 12 per cent; during this time there has been a drop in the number of smokers but an increase in the number of cigarettes smoked per person. We must be a little cautious in interpreting these facts, because many of those who have given up have been casual, non-addicted smokers, and those who have changed from high-tar to low-tar brands tend to be anxious smokers who worry about the health risks and therefore keep a careful count of the number of cigarettes they smoke.

However, there is another reason for supposing that the current policy of trying to wean smokers on to low-tar, low-nicotine brands may be tragically mistaken. In the past, many people have avoided becoming smokers because they found their first, experimental cigarettes so unpleasant. As cigarettes become milder, it is increasingly unlikely that they will put off inexperienced smokers, so a general switch to mild cigarettes may actually *increase* the number of children who take up the habit.

The only sure way to be a non-smoker is never to start. For the incorrigible addict, safer (but not safe) smoking is possible. It will not however be reached via the new smoking material as it is currently being developed, because this will be far too low on nicotine to satisfy the addicted smoker. If it is to be successful, this new material must be high on nicotine but low on tar, and the task of separating these two, though possible, will involve cigarette manufacturers in considerable expense which at present they seem unwilling to contemplate. But since the cost to the British economy in working days lost due to the effects of smoking is currently estimated to be equal to half of the tax revenue from the sale of tobacco, they might well be asked to reconsider their attitude.

17 Worrying

Of all the habits discussed in this book, I suppose that worrying comes closest to popular ideas of what psychology is about. The man in the street still regards psychologists as people who deal with madness or neurosis, and *excessive* worrying is, of course, a feature of most types of neurotic disorder. So, although I hope that the preceding chapters have shown that there is a lot more to psychology than the study of abnormal behaviour, it seems fitting to end by discussing a habit which traditionally lies at the heart of the subject.

Anxiety – a modern evil?
There are two assumptions which dominate our thinking about worrying or feeling anxious (there is no distinction between worry and anxiety in either common language or psychiatric terminology, so I shall use the terms interchangeably). The first is that worrying is a product of modern, urban society. The historian Arthur Schlesinger Jr, for example, has labelled anxiety the official emotion of our age, and there is a widespread belief that if only we could turn the clock back and recreate the Golden Age in which our ancestors lived, worry might go away. This is an attractive idea, but it is almost certainly wrong. If you list the causes of your worries, you will probably find it impossible to think of any period in the past which you can regard as less worrying than now. Changes in the nature of society have certainly exacerbated certain worries – for example, those which arise from doubt about our position in the scheme of things – but where others are concerned (infant mortality, general health and poverty) we are mollycoddled in comparison with our ancestors.

This is not the only sort of historical evidence. It is not easy to assess accurately the amount of mental illness at the present time, let alone in the past, but the calculation made by an English doctor in 1733 that nervous disorders then accounted for about a third of the illness experienced by people 'of condition' (that is, the upper classes) is very like the estimates of neurotic disorders among the general population of Britain at present – one person in three probably has first-hand experience of neurosis. Neurosis is not even a comparatively recent problem. Some 2500 years ago the Greek physician Hippocrates gave a clear description of phobias, not only of heights but of flutes! A century later, Demosthenes successfully cured a nervous tic in his shoulder by using an early form of aversion therapy, involving his sword rather than the electric shocks favoured nowadays.

Another reason for doubting whether anxiety is increased by the stresses and strains of modern urban life is that cross-cultural studies show that both the symptoms and the incidence of neurotic disorders found in Western cities are equally typical of primitive tribes, and more advanced rural communities, in Africa and Asia. So it seems that *neurotic* worrying is a world-wide problem, which has little to do with advancing culture, industrialisation, or urban living.

So far, we have been mainly concerned with excessive worrying, but it is not only neurotics who worry. The second common assumption, that worrying is necessarily a bad habit, is also quite false. At less intense levels, anxiety has great value, because worrying about the consequences of your actions often prevents you from doing things you might later regret. It also helps you to cope with trouble which can't be avoided, by taking the form of an internal monologue in which you can pursue the solution to a problem. At a time of crisis, worrying can make you face the problem which has precipitated your anxiety, and so ward off a possible breakdown. In less extreme circumstances, mild anxiety makes you more alert and energetic, and there is a great deal of experimental evidence that normally placid people perform better in a wide variety of tasks (such as speaking in public or doing an I.Q. test) when they are mildly anxious. Anxiety is regularly used in a constructive way, and even neurotic worries, which are by definition opposed to our own best interests, may not be entirely irrational. For example,

178

the most common objects of phobias (intense, uncontrollable fears of certain objects and situations) are snakes, spiders, small furry animals, darkness, large open areas and small confined spaces. All of these have, at some point in evolution, posed a genuine threat to survival, which suggests that many neurotic worries are anachronistic rather than illogical. 'Normal' worrying seems to involve the exercise of higher mental processes, while neurotic worries stem from more primitive centres of the brain. These areas may not be under voluntary control, which explains why people suffering from neurotic disorders usually have no difficulty in recognising that their behaviour is inappropriate, but are unable to change it.

Why worry?
Although it may be useful to worry, no one can pretend that it is enjoyable. The reason for this is simple: when you think about unpleasant things which may happen or find yourself back in a place where some misfortune has occurred in the past, the centres in the brain which register the experience of pain are brought into operation, even though you are not actually suffering the misfortune at that moment. This ability of the brain to remember and anticipate pain (and, similarly, pleasure) provides the biological mechanism which underpins the hedonic principle of motivation – the idea that the basic objective of everything we do is to achieve as much pleasure and as little pain as we possibly can (different people will, of course, find different things painful or pleasurable, but this in no way contradicts the hedonic principle). As a result of worrying about unpleasant things which may happen, we are often able to prevent them actually happening. So it makes sense to accept the comparatively mild unpleasantness of feeling anxious, in the hope that it will enable you to avoid greater pain later – indeed, you may subsequently feel positively good, because when you succeed in avoiding some anticipated misfortune, the 'pain centre' in the brain stops firing, and whenever this happens the corresponding 'pleasure centre' is automatically stimulated. This physiological *rebound effect* is the basis of the emotion of relief; it also explains why you feel good when you stop banging your head against a brick wall!

179

When do we first experience anxiety? According to Freud, being born is a major source of anxiety. The most influential contemporary exponent of this view is probably the Californian therapist Arthur Janov, whose primal therapy (the one where you scream) is based on the assumption that all adult neuroses can be traced back to the traumas suffered at the time of birth. However, most psychoanalysts claim that children are free from anxiety until they become old enough to appreciate the extent of their helplessness and dependence on other people. But perhaps the most important article of psychoanalytic faith is that all the neurotic worries which afflict adults have their origins in early childhood experience. There are two reasons for thinking that this belief is false. In the first place, like other species, we seem to be born with a certain number of fears (sudden changes of height, for example), while other worries such as fear of the dark and anxiety about strangers develop universally at certain points in childhood, irrespective of a child's experience, and in a way which suggests that we are genetically predisposed to have fears, and hence to worry. Moreover, many adult neuroses seem to stem from traumatic events experienced towards the end of adolescence or even later. Generally, the current view is that the importance of experiences in infancy and early childhood in determining all aspects of adult personality – including the tendency to develop neuroses – has been exaggerated.

Most psychologists would agree, however, that anxiety plays a crucial role in socialisation. Even if we accept that babies are genetically programmed to become social beings, it is difficult to see how children could learn to restrain and shape their behaviour into socially accepted patterns if they were not affected by the fear of parental disapproval or the withdrawal of love. One product of socialisation is the conscience, by which we experience guilt. Since many worries arise from feeling guilty, we can't altogether ignore the past when trying to explain what is worrying us at present.

But historical considerations only take us so far in explaining why we feel worried, or seeing what can be done to make us worry less. There are two major precipitating causes of anxiety: conflict and stress. So far as conflict is concerned, we can rarely predict the precise consequences of what we do, but as we have already seen we are blessed (or cursed) with the intellectual capacity to anticipate the advantages and disadvantages – the pleasure and the pain – which may result from any given action. We are continually having to decide between several courses of action, each of which has pros and cons, and are for ever having to resolve this state of affairs – in psychological jargon, it is known as multiple approach-avoidance conflict – which accounts for a great deal of worrying: worrying, that is, about what to do.

We also worry when things go wrong, or when life gets on top of us – a state often described by the word 'stress'. But stress, as it is used in a psychological context, has been called the most grandly imprecise term in the dictionary of science. It is rather like sin – both words are emotionally charged, both have had volumes devoted to explaining them, and both mean different things to different people. It has become fashionable to regard any circumstances which produce a physiological stress response (measured, for example, by an increase in production of the hormones adrenalin and nor-adrenalin) as sources of stress. If we follow this practice, excessive heat and cold, smoking a cigarette, watching a violent film, playing bingo or tennis, kissing passionately, having an operation, and the threat of a fight all become stressors. So do death, illness, boredom, noise, the loss of work, money problems, marital problems, retirement, and all forms of competition, conflict and uncertainty. So, although 'stress' is often used as if it were a precise clinical term, it is really nothing of the sort.

Researchers have tended to concentrate on the physical illnesses which may be precipitated by prolonged exposure to stress (ulcers, asthma, hypertension, migraine and coronary thrombosis, for example) but it may also be a potent source of anxiety. Prolonged exposure to a stressor leads to a distinctive pattern of physiological changes, the net effect of which is to prepare you for violent physical activity, but this response is a mixed blessing. It prepares you for fight or flight, neither of which is likely to be the best way of dealing with the situation which is causing you stress. What is called for is usually intellectual rather than physical energy, and although the stress hormones can help by charging you up (they may even get through to the brain and speed up your thinking) a prolonged period in which you produce high adrenalin and nor-adrenalin is physically damaging. The speed at which you resume a normal level of production of the stress hormones, when the stress is removed, is an important individual characteristic – the longer it takes, the more anxious a person you are.

Although many stress-induced worries have a rational basis, we are decidedly irrational in the way we pursue them. For example, some investigators have found the fear of death to be as strong among young adults as among the elderly; more dramatically, objective measures of anxiety show that we are no less worried an hour before having a tooth filled than we are when facing major surgery. So far as anxiety about illness is concerned, it has been suggested that the more we know about a disease, the less we fear it. But hypochondria is an occupational hazard of the medical profession: recently, an eminent English doctor refused to undergo surgery, having concluded from the diagnosis he had performed on himself that he was suffering from inoperable stomach cancer. He died, but post-mortem examination revealed that the cause of death was actually a perforated ulcer. People who live in fear of becoming ill are actually no more likely to take effective prophylactic measures, like being vaccinated or making sure that they have regular check-ups, than those who are not concerned about their health.

How do we deal with worries? Where possible, we organise our lives so that we steer clear altogether of certain situations which we find alarming: people who hate flying may often be able to travel by some other means of transport, for example. Alternatively, we try to convince ourselves that we are not really worried at all, but such a denial can leave us dangerously unprepared if there is in fact good reason to worry. The repression of specific worries can lead to the clinical condition of free-floating anxiety – a feeling of intense fear and general unease, which cannot be traced to any specific source – while unresolved worries remain a nagging source of stress, which, as we have seen, can make us physically ill (this is known as *somatised* anxiety). Repressing anxiety affects different types of person in different ways: it has been suggested that highly authoritarian people become more prone to physical disorders, while those with a liberal outlook are more likely to suffer from some psychological disorder. It is much safer to seek temporary relief from anxiety by indulging in a variety of *coping behaviours*. Many of the commonest items in our behavioural repertoire – smoking, drinking, sleeping, eating, taking strenuous exercise and day-dreaming, to name but a few – can help to reduce anxiety to a level at which it is no longer debilitating, and thus put us in a fit state to cope with whatever is bothering us, in a rational manner. It is only when such crutches fail that anxiety threatens to become a clinical problem.

Who worries?
Of course, some people worry more than others, whatever the situation. So far we have been discussing the *state* of anxiety, which is largely the product of events and circumstances. But worrying is also a personality *trait*, or individual characteristic, partly determined by the genes you inherit, which is why the same experience makes one person worry more than another. The likelihood of someone having a neurotic breakdown is determined jointly by how prone he is to anxiety and how much stress there is in his life – it will take less life-stress to push a naturally anxious person over the top. This is underlined by the fact that people rarely suffer a neurotic breakdown for the first time late in life, although stress-inducing events may become even more frequent as we get older.

The tendency to worry also varies between the sexes – women have been found to be more anxious than men, wherever the comparison has been made – and between nations. Taking the incidence of suicide, alcoholism, mental illness, heart disease, hypertension and calorie intake (we know that the more anxious we are, the less we tend to eat) as measures of anxiety, we can produce a league-table of anxiety levels in eighteen developed countries in Western and Northern Europe, Japan and the U.S., which begins as follows:

1 Japan
2 West Germany

3 Austria
4 Italy
5 France
6 Belgium
7 Holland

Sweden lies twelfth in the table, the U.S. fifteenth, Britain seventeenth and Eire eighteenth. Perhaps the most surprising feature of this table is how little support it offers for the widely held belief that economic problems are a major cause of anxiety: the two most anxious nations, Japan and Germany, had far more flourishing economies than the least anxious, Britain and Eire, throughout the period from which the figures were taken. The reasons behind these national differences are not yet fully understood: the weather probably plays a part – hot summers and frequent storms have both been linked with anxiety – and we know that the more facilities available for dealing with mental illness in a given area, the more mental illness will occur.

Since the tendency to worry is affected by such factors as personality, sex and nationality, it is a mistake to try and apply general statements about the causes or the nature of anxiety to yourself or anyone else without taking careful account of individual characteristics. What you find rather exciting may terrify someone else. Remember also that a moderate level of anxiety may galvanise you into achieving more. Studies show that successful people in many walks of life score higher than average on objective tests of anxiety, so I repeat: worrying is not necessarily a bad habit.

Neurotic worrying

It is difficult to decide at what point worrying ceases to be 'normal', and becomes neurotic. You may not share the depth of Freud's pessimism ('Life as we find it is too hard for us; it entails too much pain, too many disappointments, impossible tasks'), but there is clearly plenty to worry about – people do get seriously ill, plans go awry, and planes sometimes crash. Neurosis is a fairly loose concept, used to describe behaviour which is associated with strong emotional feelings, which is maladaptive, and which the sufferer realises is absurd or irrelevant but he is powerless to change. The key notion is

184

maladaptiveness: anxiety is judged to be pathological when it prevents us leading a normal existence. We can manage quite well without travelling in planes or lifts, and an evening out isn't spoiled by the fact that we can't leave the house without triple-checking that the front-door is locked. Such quirks are widespread among people who never need to go to a doctor to complain about their 'nerves', and there is no difficulty in distinguishing between them and the behaviour of someone suffering from, say, severe agoraphobia or an obsessional compulsion. The former may be unable ever to leave the house, the latter incapable of taking a bath in less than seven hours, and neither will be able to lead a normal life.

In its extreme form, anxiety may be experienced either as the generalised, free-floating state mentioned earlier, or it may be focused specifically on certain objects or situations. Most people have experienced the former – the taut muscles and dry mouth accompanied by a feeling of agitation, dread or even panic – and mild phobias are also very common among 'normal' people. As any sufferer will know, the experience of extreme tension or anxiety is very unpleasant and frightening, and there is little immediate comfort to be gained from being able either to identify its cause or to perceive that it is groundless. But it is important to realise that anxiety does not drive one mad, and it may be reassuring to know that two out of every three people suffering from extreme neurosis recover completely without any professional assistance whatsoever. Phobias and compulsions are less likely to disappear without professional aid, but the technique of behaviour therapy, which treats neurotic symptoms as bad habits which must be unlearned and replaced by more adaptive forms of behaviour, is highly – though not completely – successful in dealing with these conditions.

There are also a variety of drugs which can alleviate the effects of anxiety – actually, alcohol is as effective as any, and it tastes more pleasant than most. Drugs don't *cure* neurosis, but they can make life more bearable until such time as the condition has receded, either as a result merely of the passage of time, or by the sufferer's own determination, helped by relatives, friends, or – if these fail – professional advice. More drastic medical techniques, like electric shock treatment and even brain surgery, are also sometimes used to treat neurosis, and those who can afford to may seek the help of a psychotherapist.

But since neurosis is a behavioural rather than a medical problem, most forms of treatment are just palliatives which help to put the sufferer into a frame of mind in which he can cure himself. If you or someone close to you seems to be threatened by a breakdown, you will find Stuart Sutherland's book *Breakdown* immensely helpful. This is an experimental psychologist's account of his own breakdown in which he evaluates the alternative forms of treatment available, from a scientific point of view but with his own experience of them in mind. He concludes that no single form of treatment is suitable for all sufferers, and warns against therapists who try to convince you otherwise. You should find a therapist who is prepared to try a variety of approaches to your problem. The most helpful thing you can do for someone else undergoing a breakdown is to persuade him that the future offers some hope, by reminding him of his past achievements and assuring him that his condition is only temporary. The conviction that you will never recover is a symptom of severe depression, and it is not borne out by the figures. Remember that most people suffering from extreme neurosis recover completely, even without treatment, and nine out of ten patients admitted to psychiatric hospitals for all forms of mental illness are released within a year.

In conclusion, we all worry, and would be in poor shape if we did not. Worrying keeps us out of trouble and it energises us. It can also help us to recover from, for example, bereavement, by helping us come to terms with reality; in such circumstances, dosing ourselves with tranquillisers may actually be counter-productive. More generally, it is difficult to see how we could ever make social or intellectual progress if we did not worry to some extent. On balance, worrying is a useful habit, and perhaps the time to get worried is when you notice that you have stopped worrying.

Bibliography

A more detailed treatment of some of the topics dicussed in this book can be found in the following:

Ardrey, R. *The Territorial Imperative* (Atheneum Press, 1966).
Argyle, M. *Social Interaction* (Methuen, 1969).
Argyle, M. *Bodily Communication* (Methuen, 1975).
Argyle, M. and Beit-Hallahmi, B. *The Social Psychology of Religion* (Routledge & Kegan Paul, 1975).
Baddeley, A. D. *The Psychology of Memory* (Harper & Row, 1976).
Birenbaum, A. and Sagarin, E. *People in Places* (Nelson, 1973).
Brown, L. R. *Ideology* (Penguin, 1973).
Brown, L. R. *Psychology and Religion* (Penguin, 1973).
Bruner, J. S., Jolly, A. and Sylva, K. *Play: Its Role in Evolution and Development* (Penguin, 1976).
Byrne, D. *The Attraction Paradigm* (Academic Press, 1972).
Carruthers, M. *The Western Way of Death* (Davis-Poynter, 1974).
Christie, R. and Geiss, F. L. *Studies in Machiavellianism* (Academic Press, 1970).
Clarke, A. M. and Clarke, A. D. B. *Early Experience* (Open Books, 1976).
Cook, M. *Interpersonal Perception* (Penguin, 1971).
Davies, D. R. and Shackelton, V. J. *Psychology and Work* (Methuen, 1975).
Duck, S. *Personal Relationships and Personal Constructs* (Wiley, 1973).
Evans, P. *Motivation* (Methuen, 1975).
Eysenck, H. J. *You and Neurosis* (Temple Smith, 1977).
Fast, J. *Body Language* (Evans, 1970).
Fisher, A. C. *The Psychology of Sport* (Mayfield, 1976).
Freedman, J. L. *Crowding and Behaviour* (Freeman, 1975).
Goffman, E. *Frame Analysis* (Harper & Row, 1974).
Goffman, E. *Presentation of Self in Everyday Life* (Pelican, 1975).
Gruneberg, M. M. *Job Satisfaction* (Macmillan, 1976).
Hall, E. T. *The Silent Language* (Doubleday, 1959).
Hinde, R. *Non-verbal Communication* (Cambridge University Press, 1972).

Lee, S. G. M. and Mayes, A. R. *Dreams and Dreaming*
(Penguin, 1973).
Lee, T. *Psychology and the Environment* (Methuen, 1976).
Lorenz, K. *On Aggression* (Methuen, 1966).
Maccoby, E. and Jacklin, C. *The Psychology of Sex Differences*
(Oxford University Press, 1975).
McLelland, D. C. and Winter, D. G. *Motivating Economic
Achievement* (Free Press, 1969).
Mercer, C. *Living in Cities* (Penguin, 1975).
Morris, D. *The Naked Ape* (Cape, 1967).
Newson, J. and Newson, E. *Four Years Old in an Urban Community*
(Penguin, 1970).
Richards, M. P. M. *The Integration of a Child into a Social World*
(Cambridge University Press, 1974).
Schachter, S. *Emotion, Obesity and Crime* (Academic Press, 1971).
Singer, J. L. *The Child's World of Make-believe*
(Academic Press, 1973).
Sommer, R. *Personal Space* (Prentice-Hall, 1969).
Sutherland, S. *Breakdown* (Weidenfeld & Nicolson, 1976).
Swingle, P. G. *Social Psychology in Everyday Life* (Penguin, 1973).
Tuck, M. *How Do We Choose?* (Methuen, 1976).
Warr, P. and Wall, T. *Work and Well-being* (Penguin, 1975).
Wilson, G. and Nias, D. *Love's Mysteries* (Open Books, 1976).

Index

189

Drunken driving, effect of smoking on, 169–70

Eating: and anxiety, 183; as celebration, 36–7; as habit, 34–5; as source of conflict between parents and children, 37; children's attitudes to, 38; conventions, 36; importance of early experiences, 37; over-eating *see* Obesity; physiology of, 33–4; sociological aspects of, 7, 35, 36; under-eating, 43
Ego-identity, 152
Ekman, Paul, 64, 112, 113
Electric shock treatment, 185
Electroencephalogram (EEG), 45, 46, 48, 171
Eyewitness evidence, 100, 101, 103
Eysenck, Hans, 172

'Face', 144, 145, 146, 147
Fast, Julius, 123
Flats, and relation to crime, 22, 23
Football, 28, 29, 131, 132, 133–4, 142
Ford, Henry, 76
Fox, Robin, 147
Freud, Sigmund: on anxiety of birth, 180; on 'bobbing and weaving', 159; on children and eating, 37; on God as fantasised parent-figure, 152; on inside lavatories, 29–30; on 'leakage', 143; on the pain of life, 184; on religion and neurosis, 151, 154
Friendship: need for, 67–8, 74; physical factors of, 72–3; short- and long-term, 70–2; similarity–complementarity in, 68–72

Games: children's, 138–9; cooperative, 123; factors of success in, 132; laboratory, 124–6, 130; life-, 122, 123, 142–3; marital, 123; non-cooperative,

123; non-zero sum, 123; psychology in, 132, 133; zero-sum, 123; *see also* Sport

Hall, Edward, 11, 13, 14
Hedonic principle, 167, 179
Home, 28, 29, 30, 37
Honour, concept of, 147, 148
Hypnosis: and obesity, 42; and sleep, 45, 57
Hypochondria, 182

Identical twins, 34
Identification parades, 100, 101–3
Industrial negotiation, art of, 85–7
Insomnia, 23, 56–7
Insults: cultural and historical differences affecting, 147–9; definition of, 144; non-verbal, 145; reactions to, 145–6; subtle forms of, 147, 149–50
Interviews, 13, 15, 25; board, 117, 118; group assessment, 117, 119; impressions at beginning of, 115; one-to-one, 117, 119, 120; tips for interviewers, 120–1; psychiatric, 142
I.Q., 72, 114, 130, 178

Janov, Arthur, 180
Jehovah's Witnesses, 156–7
Job enrichment, 76, 81, 83
Judging: as a skill, 112–13, 116–17; distortions in, 115–16; in everyday life, 112–17; in interviews, 117–21; in trial by jury, 110–12; use of stereotypes in, 113–14

Landmarks, psychological importance of, 27
Laughter, 60–61, 64, 145
Loneliness, 16, 23
Losing, 130–1
Lorenz, Konrad, 10, 133, 134
Lung cancer, 167, 168, 170, 171, 175

Schachter, Stanley, 41
Schizophrenia, 14, 22, 141, 156–7
Sex differences: in aggression,
24–5, 129; in anxiety, 183; in fear
of success, 128–9; in handling
people, 129; in judging character,
116; in laboratory games, 126;
in management techniques, 85;
in need for personal space, 14;
in need to achieve, 128; in
negotiation, 87; in obesity, 38–39;
in pedestrian behaviour, 165;
in power seeking, 127; in
smoking, 172
Shopping, 92–5; see also Buying
Short-sightedness, related to
intelligence, 114
Sleep: afternoon nap, benefits of,
35, 50; effects of lack of, 50; and
exercise, 50–51; in animals, 47,
52; insomnia, 56–7; need for,
46–9; physiology of, 44–6;
popular beliefs about, 44, 46, 50;
rapid eye movement (REM):
46–51 passim, and dreaming,
51–6; slow-wave sleep (SWS),
45–51 passim; social conventions
concerning, 56
Sleeping pills, 57
Smiling, 112–13, 143, 148; as
influence on feelings, 66; as
NVC, 58–9; and deception,
61–2; different types of, 59;
importance of: in adulthood,
58–62, in infancy, 62–4; and
tension, 63, 64, 65; universality
of, 65–6
Smoking: and anxiety, 172–3;
effects: on alcohol level, 169–70,
on memory, 107, 170,
physiological, 168–9, 170, 171,
172–3; giving up, 174–6;
infringing hedonic principle,
167; and lung cancer, 167, 168,
170–1; reasons for, 171–2, 173–4;
types, 173–4; see also
Cigarettes, Nicotine

Sport, 123, 131–4; see also Games
Staring, 143, 145, 147, 148
Suicide, 22, 27, 129, 183

Territoriality, 9–11, 16–18
Tickling, 64, 65
Toilet training, 29–30, 37
Traffic accidents, 23, 98–100

Walking: alone, 163, 166; as an
accomplishment, 159, 160, 162;
as index of pace of life, 162;
characteristic types of, 160;
conventions governing, 163–5;
for pleasure, 159; in a group,
163
Weight, maximum desirable, 38,
39
Winning: and need for
achievement, 125. 127, 128;
and need for power, 125, 127,
129; non-verbal, 123;
psychology of, 126–7, 131–3;
see also Games,
Machiavellianism
Work: attitudes towards, 75–6,
77–8; motivation for, 76–8;
self-image in, 77; stressful types
of, 78–80; see also Industrial
negotiation, Job enrichment,
Management
Worker participation, 81–2